To the sweetest couple I
know. Welcome to the family!

D1603308

(RE)BORN AGAIN

CRUCIFYING CHRISTENDOM
& RESURRECTING A RADICAL

Christopher VanHall

TABLE OF CONTENTS

ABOUT THIS BOOK 1

PROLOGUE 3

CHAPTER 1: HYPOCRITES... 17

CHAPTER 2: SCALES... 29

CHAPTER 3: GOSPELS... 49

CHAPTER 4: IDOLS.. 73

CHAPTER 5: SAMARITANS.. 87

CHAPTER 6: SODOMITES.. 99

CHAPTER 7: EDEN.. 121

CHAPTER 8: CAPTIVES... 139

CHAPTER 9: CENTURIONS 165

CHAPTER 10: TRANSFIGURATION.................................... 187

EPILOGUE 203

FURTHER READING 205

SPECIAL THANKS 207

NOTES..215

ABOUT THIS BOOK

This memoir is isolated to a few significant events that encouraged my evolution as a Christian and as a pastor. You will find memories, ministry breakthroughs, and perhaps most importantly theological discoveries that led me away from toxic fundamentalism. Please note that I am not an accredited authority. Though I have been employed in Church my entire adult life, and I am somewhat of a leading voice in certain forums, I am no scholar. In light of this, I will share information regarding every controversial topic that I cover from individuals who are superb theologians. I encourage all to read the books recommended in the "Further Reading" section of this literary work as well. Finally, I challenge you to question every topic I discuss in this body of text. For without questioning and doubt, our faith is both stagnant and boring.

Each chapter within this publication is a sequential step forward in my life journey, and in my embrace of progressive Christianity. Some folks may find the early stages of my career troubling, and their sense of frustration with my past will be justifiable. In the early chapters of this book, I simply am being honest about my ethics and theology during these points in time. Regrettably, my transformation was not instantaneous. It took many eye-opening encounters, years of research, and moments of pause for self-examination to get to where I am today. I am not proud of the person I projected in my former life, but I am committed to honest transparency for my audience. I apologize for the pain that those views have caused in the past and for the pain I caused when I held them. I forever am committed to fighting the influences of exclusive manifestos in our culture until my dying breath.

My social, political, and theological outlook is currently characterized by positions such as feminism, Native rights activism, anti-racism (Black Lives Matter), sexual liberty, nonviolent subversion, open and affirming LGBTQ+ theology, embracing evolution as fact, encouraging the pursuit of new scientific knowledge, environmentalism, economic justice, social justice, and the legalization of recreational drugs, etc.

You may disagree with any or all of the above, but don't you want to know how I got there?

Christian readers, beware. I use the term "fuck" and I sprinkle other colorful four-letter adjectives (aka sentence enhancers) throughout this narrative.

Non-Christian readers, beware. There are some theological terms and phrases with which you may not be familiar. Fear not. These definitions and explanations are just a Google search away. Now, buckle up and enjoy the ride.

Grace and peace,

Christopher VanHall

PROLOGUE

There I sat, and fading before me was the most influential figure of my entire existence. The person whom I had turned to when I needed an escape from a troublesome childhood. The one who loved me with kind words of affirmation and whose actions consistently displayed affection. There was the only positive role model I had, my Grandpa, lying in a hospital bed, lungs desperately gasping for air.

I settled at the foot of the bed hopelessly in the midst of this solemn reminder of finite mortality with virtually nothing to do, but observe this catastrophic departure from my world.

My grandpa was unable to move or speak while trapped inside a once strong body. By the time our family had arrived at our grandpa's bedside, this once towering specimen could no longer blink, but could only stare with dilated and motionless pupils fixated on the ceiling while wearing a face devoid of emotion. There we gathered to mourn, and there we remained without any evidence that we were witnessing cognizance, and with no indication of an awareness to our presence.

My tears streamed from cheek to floor, as recollections of spending every weekend at my grandparents' house saturated my thoughts. I distinctly recalled a masculine voice teasing me for my inadequate taste in Saturday morning cartoons as my grandparents forced themselves to watch atrocious animation in order to spend quality time with their grandchild. I remember my grandpa letting me drive through the front yard when I was in kindergarten, while holding my tiny frame high over the steering column. I remembered spending innumerable hours on various lakes fishing for bluegill, catfish, and warmouth bass. I dwelled on how much everyone loved being in the company of such an extraordinary soul no matter their circumstance. This wondrous luminary had the ability to produce joy in every arena, and this rare gift followed in tow as if it were stitched to the shadow my grandpa cast.

This crucial character was meant to contribute to many future chapters of my life story. We had devised our expectations, and I wasn't prepared to bid farewell anytime soon. There was still a speech to be recited at my wedding. There was supposed to be a grand introduction given to my newborn children one day. And then, when the time was right, my grandpa would live with me when home care became necessary. Terminal cancer was never part of this world to come, and it shattered every calculation of how I thought my life would unfold. Far too much time had been ripped from our clutches due to the unexpected onset of this aggressive illness.

This day of remembrance was drenched in tragedy, and reeked of unfairness, and to make matters worse, I was the cause.

Or at least I believed I was.

"Why isn't my prayer working?" I questioned in desperation, trying to assess my life and unearth some buried sin from my past that was hindering my teenage prayers for my grandpa's healing from coming to fruition.

"What is stopping this miracle?" I pondered furiously as I confessed every detestable act defined by evangelicalism from memory.

The white lies I consistently told to my parents.

My secret disdain for certain classmates who did not fit within my unachievable criteria for being "saved."

The erotic sexual fantasies I frequently had about multiple teachers at my high school.

I confessed all of it, and at this death bed pledged an oath of true repentance due to these manifestations of my "impure heart."

To my discouragement, I watched as respiration continued to become increasingly strenuous. My thoughts and prayers were yielding absolutely no measurable assistance in stabilizing my grandpa.

I reached out and placed my hands on my grandpa's ice cold ankles as I sat weeping in despair. I closed my eyes again in an attempt to negotiate life with God.

"Lord, whatever my sin is, I am sorry. I regret 'backsliding,' but I beseech you, please remove this cancer. Restore this vessel. I will forever be your servant, and I will submit myself to mission work in whatever war-torn country you select. I only ask that you have mercy on us now. I will die to every ambition I will ever have, wholly submit my will to your own, but please do not take my grandpa from me. "

I repeated differing variations of my request hundreds of times. This repetition continued for hours with unchanging results.

I even tried to alter my approach.

"Perhaps I am communicating with the wrong entity?" I speculated. After all, according to the excessively sweaty Pentecostal minister who preached to me every Sunday morning, sickness and disease were a result of "demonic attacks."

"I rebuke you, in the name of the Father, the Son, and the Holy Spirit. You have no dominion here! I demand that you leave my presence. I cast you out of this body, and place a hedge of protection around this weakened spirit," I whispered.

I was unsure of the benefit that this heavenly landscaping would provide, but my pastor used these "hedges of protection" often when praying for sick congregants. I imagined that this ethereal shrubbery must be quite intimidating, so I wanted to utilize it. Despite my efforts to engage in "spiritual warfare," nothing changed. There was no visual confirmation that vitality was returning to this declining figure.

Scientifically speaking, my grandpa was losing a second bout with cancer. Unfortunately for our family, there wasn't a responsive reaction to treatment. In fact, the treatment itself was so toxic it destroyed any ability for vital organs to recover.

Theologically speaking, I believed this affliction to be my fault, and sadly I realized that I was running out of divine beings with whom to barter life. There was only one entity left with whom to plead, so I leaned down and whispered, "Please don't go."

But the certainty of death was inescapable.

I bitterly accepted this inevitability and clung to my grandpa for what felt like hours. The hardest part about this wasn't that I couldn't feel the reciprocation of my embrace at this moment. It was knowing that I would never feel it again.

Words I severely wished to share lodged in my throat. No matter my effort, it seemed impossible to force them to my lips. I longed for the courage to express my love one last time, but I couldn't do it. This final farewell was far from fair, and I was far from well.

My grandma, with streams of tears pouring over the sheets, leaned over to me, and said these words through a cracking voice: "Your grandpa is not going to pass until you say goodbye. Christopher, you have to say it is okay to go, and that you will be fine."

If my inability to say goodbye was causing death to linger, then I could not bear the burden of causing any more suffering. It was hard enough believing myself to be the reason for this entire situation.

The most painful phrase I have ever uttered to this very day is, "Goodbye, I love you so much. I'll always love you. You can go."

Seconds later there were a few slow breaths, and then a once struggling chest lay still. My heart was decimated. We mourned together until funeral services arrived, and my grandfather was taken out of the room.

I forced my way through a barrage of family members in my grandpa's bedroom attempting to comfort me. I opened the screen door, walked outside, and found myself sobbing in the shade of an oak tree. To my left a stone bird bath swarmed with feathered creatures that were unbothered by my recent experience of loss. Hummingbirds, cardinals, and bluejays landed and bathed within arm's reach, but I could see no beauty in their presence. Admiring the miracle of life after witnessing death felt like an insult.

The melody of wind chimes echoed around me as I hung my head in disbelief.

My filthy, wretched soul had done this.

If I had just prayed more,

or if I didn't have impure thoughts,

or if I had tithed more money to the church instead of going out with my friends,

or if I had read my Bible frequently,

or if I had respected my parents' wishes,

or if I didn't lie to my first period teacher about why I was late every single day,

or if I didn't curse under my breath when I stubbed my toe,

...Then the most precious hero of my childhood would have been miraculously healed. I was sure of it. I truly believed in my heart of hearts that I was responsible for this day.

My sins had made me an accomplice to murder.

<hr />

My reaction to this tragedy is what the fruit of toxic theology looks like. It creeps into dire situations, buries its roots into the weakened spirit of the broken, spreads its seeds in the tattered minds of the innocent, and renders the foundation of its victim more damaged than it was before.

I truly wish that this event was a catalyst for my exodus from evangelical belief.

It wasn't.

There was no inkling of conversion immediately after my grandfather's death to a different interpretation of scripture. There was no sudden monumental shift in how I understood the sovereignty of God. There was no instantaneous transition to progressive hermeneutics. This was not a happening that spurred questions about my understanding of the sacred texts. I wish it had, but it didn't.

Instead, I drew closer to the source of my inner turmoil. I doubled down on my commitment to repent of my sinful ways, unknowingly embracing the flames that previously scorched my soul.

My assumptions about God and the Scriptures had subjected me to a lifestyle of guilt, loss, and self-shaming. In my understanding, I was a disgusting sinner in the eyes of God. I was deserving of death and eternal torment with grace only bestowed on me by reciting a magic prayer, and repenting from sinful behavior that (unknown to me at that time) may, or may not have actually been in the Bible. As a young person devoted to the cause of nurturing evangelicalism, I knew that there was some unconfessed sin in my life that had caused God to ignore my plea for my grandpa's healing. After all, my pastor said that God's ear was muffled to the prayers of the "wicked," and I was taught that wickedness was grafted to my being from the moment I was born. God could not save my grandpa because, according to every sermon I had heard, I was not worth saving based on my own merit. The Bible that was projected from the pulpit made it clear to the sixteen-year-old version of me, that I had been an active participant in my grandpa's death because of my inherently sinful nature.

This detrimental understanding of the Bible, and beliefs of similar impact are the reason I am writing this book.

Stories like mine aren't uncommon. In truth, many readers may find themselves skimming over this prologue because it is nothing unique from their own agonizing experience in the Church.

(The last sentence may actually be the most discouraging statement in this entire memoir.)

I have found that many recovering evangelicals have left the Church for many reasons. Some understandably cannot stomach the hypocrisy, bigotry, cruelty, and corruption in a movement that was historically intended to combat those very ideals. Throughout history, Christianity as a whole has been a global arbiter of darkness. Thus, many have found that "church" is a dirty word.

Some may feel that "church" is more authentically expressed in public service. They encounter the Divine in feeding the hungry and in environmental efforts.

Perhaps some have seen that spiritual "community" can be experienced more tangibly in a bar or a coffee shop than in a boring presentation on Sunday mornings.

There are those who simply cannot accept their former nature when confronted with the qualities of the Christian Right (which are often neither Christian nor right), knowing that at one point in time they themselves nourished this oppressive institution with their time and talent.

There also is the problem of clergy leaving their collars behind out of exhaustion. Many former leaders in Christendom are burnt out from attempting to lead their parish in embracing models that are dynamic, refreshing, and relevant. In the process they have continuously failed to get their congregants to let go of irrelevant traditions, toxic theology, and dated methodology.

Or perhaps their reasons are a combination of the above. In my own reality, it has been a combination of all of the above. I justifiably had the desire to flee from the church early on in my career, but I would soon discover that there is a choice beyond abandonment.

We can be a solution to the problem of an abusive institution.

In contrast, by leaving the Church, we give our permission for the problematic realities of Christendom to endure unchallenged.

Our resignation is an accessory to the continuation of dogmatic affliction.

Our indifference can no longer stand if the authentic directive of Jesus is to be reborn. This overdue revival will not come without opposition, or cost. Those in seats of power within the confines of unjust religious authority will ridicule their enemy viciously, and publicly. They will label those who oppose their preposterous inter-pretations as "blasphemous" at every turn. I am certain of this as this heinous strategy has been done by me and to me at differing points of my own spiritual journey. Still, we cannot be deterred by protests or attacks on our character if the church is to shed its cur-rent diseased and dying identity. We must confront these extremists and cling to their labels of heresy proudly. They are badges of honor and milestones of progress.

After all, our faith is constructed entirely of ancient lessons from a "blasphemous" Rabbi.

For far too long the traitor that the world calls "Church" has gone uncontested. All the while conservative Christianity has remained in the front row, wearing a "We're #1" foam finger, on the wrong side of history.

I'd argue that a little "heresy" in the eyes of a nefarious institution is necessary.

If the Gospel of Jesus is going to have impact in modern application, then it is time to place irrelevant traditions and tarnished systems of belief in the grave so that the historically radical directive of a Jewish, nonviolent, subversive rabbi named Jesus can be resurrected.

That directive is this:

The God of scripture is opposed to any system of law and order that survives by utilizing hierarchical values to elevate the status of some by lowering the societal value of many.

We see this theme emerge as early as Genesis.

The Torah contains many stories that display the dichotomy between the gods of empire and the tribal god "Elohim."

Later in Genesis, that distinction between gods is further expounded upon when Abraham feels led to offer a human sacrifice, and Abraham believes Isaac must be slaughtered to please this new God. So Abraham sets out on a solemn journey only to discover that, strangely, this God doesn't require human sacrifice. This praxis was unlike the celestial beings worshipped in Babylon. The Babylonians worshiped gods that occasionally required the slaughter of innocents as an act of devotion by pledging fealty in blood-soaked worship.

But this God of Abraham was different. This God is on our side.

The depiction of this good and just deity continues in the conflict between Moses and Egypt in the book of Exodus. Egypt enslaved the people of ancient Israel. The Israelites worshipped the God of Abraham. They could remember stories of this God of love and justice while they were forced to bow to the desires of Pharaoh. Pharaoh, for all intents and purposes, was an emperor worshipped by the Egyptians as a living god, and this god of Egypt was far from being good, or just. Pharaoh oppressed the Judean tribe, and slaughtered those who stood in Egypt's path. Then, in the wake of tyranny, something marvelous occurs.

The Hebrew God "YHWY" frees the oppressed from the clutches of empire.

Are you seeing this common theme of scripture yet?

Fast-forward many centuries, and enter Jesus.

Jesus was a Middle Eastern Jewish Rabbi who stood against another false supremacy, the empire of Rome. Once again, in the timeline of biblical history, there is an authority oppressing the Jewish people. Only this time empire also had found its way into their temple as well. Yet death and principalities do not have the final word. Using Christ's methods of subversion, the early church eventually crumbled both shrine and state, ending the rule of their overlords.

I know you see the theme now.

Fast-forward a couple thousand years to this very moment. Christendom and government have been in bed together for, well, centuries. This hellish coalition has left mountains of skulls, rivers of blood, and acres of chains in the wake of its conquest for dominance and resources.

It is no secret to the global community that Christendom is experiencing an identity crisis itself. Would-be champions of the cause are denying that the church is a viable means of revolution. They are doing so for all the right reasons. In truth, it is not the teachings of Jesus that people are fleeing. It is the imperial values that were assimilated into Christian theology dating back to Rome's adoption of the faith.

The same imperial values that landed Jesus on a cross.

The same imperial values from which Moses freed the Jewish people.

The same imperial values that Jewish people opposed in Babylon when compiling the creation poem in the Torah.

Those same values now have merged with our faith and are using the Scriptures as a vehicle to carry out destructive agendas, and it is time to abandon those values and restore a new age of love, justice, and equality.

The Church has forgotten its purpose and replaced its historical mandate with ridiculous customs and beliefs that are far from biblical. If we can illuminate the dichotomy between evangelical messiah and historical Jesus within our communities, then perhaps we can take our rightful place in the frontlines of the resistance and be the collective catalyst for change that a broken world has been longing for.

If we can identify the misguided views of what Christians believe that the Bible says, by clarifying what the Bible actually says, then I believe the church will become an unstoppable expanding force of virtue and equity.

For this to happen, the Church must first be reborn.

This book is about my own rebirth. It is about how I discovered the hijacking of Christianity by nationalism and details the dilemma that this knowledge caused while I was employed by congregations within evangelicalism. It has specific memories of the challenges that emerged with this knowledge. It tells stories of wandering in my own spiritual wilderness and contains lessons that I learned on the path to losing my religion while discovering a new Jesus.

The real Jesus.

This story details moments when I began to embrace ancient traditions of speaking truth to power. It speaks of my own struggles in preaching freedom from institutional polity, and explains my vexations in trying to convert those that these leaders have influenced for generations.

The following chapters are accounts, and field notes, in rediscovering contextual biblical teachings. Within these pages are my own imperfect attempts to creatively rebirth the movement that began long before, and continued well after, a troublemaking Rabbi named Jesus emerged from a place called Nazareth.

This is my death, birth, and new life. May it help you find yours.

HYPOCRITES

"No! We need all the stage lights to be shades of blue for this song. Not red!" I demanded. "Blue light delivers a passionate emotional response during slower songs. These songs are ballads, y'all, not club remixes. Red lights at this point of the service will alter the entire flow of worship. Red lights are too intense.

"Y'all, how many times do I have to say it? We only use red lights for the upbeat songs. Period!"

I ran my fingers furiously through my long, dense curly locks and continued my tirade.

"It is like I am asking y'all to watch *Old Yeller* with me and you want to watch *Scarface*. Wait, that is a bad metaphor, but you know what I mean."

They clearly didn't understand what I meant.

"Anyhow, the point is that I really need y'all to read the article on light therapy that I emailed you weeks ago."

The stage lights flickered frantically from red to blue as I finished scolding my music team.

The band commenced to play with impeccable precision. Our musical team was composed of (but not limited to) a bass player who had recorded with Hendrix, a drummer who could play keyboard and kit simultaneously, a flutist who could shift to turntables at a moment's notice, two phenomenal electric guitarists, and several angelic vocalists who easily could be top contenders on *The Voice*. To this day, I have not played on a stage with this much raw talent.

It was the early 2000s and I was one of three music directors at a large fundamentalist church in the Bible Belt. It was our weekly Thursday night rehearsal for our Sunday service. It was an exciting week for us. We had purchased another light system for approximately $35,000 to complement our church performance of Jesus walking on water. These expenses for our productions were far from uncommon for our church.

In the corner of the auditorium, our production crew was finishing the final touches on a sailboat frame that they spent all week fashioning to a motorized scissor lift for the actors who were playing the twelve disciples to drive through the auditorium during their performance.

Prior to rehearsal, we had been filling a massive tented area located behind our stage with smoke from low density fog machines. In theory, when the sealed entrance of the tent was opened, it would quickly flood the sanctuary floor with a thick layer of fog. The smoke in combination with our new LED light system would be quite a treat. Our newly purchased luminescence came equipped with a setting that could mimic a shimmering surface of water. Our hope for the coming worship service was that once these new lights hit the auditorium seating, their aquatic-themed special effects would reflect on the top layer of the low density fog so that it would give the audience the illusion of being seated on top of a massive body of water. This, of course, was beneficial, since they were to witness our subpar theatrics of Peter and Jesus taking a stroll on the sea.

"Don't forget right after the fourth song we need the lights completely dead. I want them cut off instantaneously," I demanded. "We need an immediate pitch black transition to the skit. Then I need row A of the stage lights to mimic lighting. That means one of you is going to have to operate the light board manually between the clashes of thunder on the audio clip. The mp3 of a thunderstorm is in the flash drive by the mixer. Have it queued up and ready to go the moment the room is dark. I want every sub-woofer cranked. We want the congregation to feel like they are in this storm, y'all."

In a lofted area positioned in the back of the sanctuary, we placed two volunteers with buckets of water. During worship they would be adjacent to giant industrial fans above the auditorium-style seating. When the storm scene commenced, the fans would be turned to their highest setting. Then our team would dump Slurpee-size cups of water in front of the high velocity blades to mimic rain falling on the audience.

As complex as the components of this performance was, it did not hold a candle to our most elaborate theatrical production. Earlier that year, we had crafted a ten-foot Goliath costume. All characteristics of this prosthetic philistine costume appeared proportionate, and not as if it was just an actor walking around on stilts. When Goliath walked across the stage, we synced the giant's steps to an audio track, and cranked the audio system full blast and played sound effects comparable to a Brachiosaurus strolling through our temple. We had a teenager in the youth department portray the young David and battle with the giant onstage. When David released a plastic rock from a sling, Goliath fell off the stage and into a foam pit behind several fake boulders. The moment our obnoxiously massive portrayal of the Philistine warrior landed, the room shook with a crash, and stagehands tossed papier-mâché rubble onto the crowd from the loft.

In another production, we placed hand-painted foam boulders into electronically activated party balloon nets for our pastor's teaching series of the book of Judges. When Samson stood between two fabricated pillars on center stage and shoved the two props outward, they shifted and cracked. The sound of massive rocks crumbling filled the room. Lights flashed and the foam rubble we painted was released from the nets onto the crowd.

We had garage doors installed behind both sides of the sanctuary stage. We utilized these entrances for horses, tractors, and cars for skits that required vehicles.

In the business of "The Jesus Show," we were part of a rising elite.

In the formative years of my career, this was just another day at the office. I gladly spent countless hours severely underpaid in order to nurture this organization that reflected what I believed church was meant to be. A grand production.

At the time, my compromised understanding of spiritual community was that Christianity was meant to be a massive performance, and the more talent and complexity that was presented on Sundays the more aware the congregation would be of God's "anointing" on that community.

These gimmicks were important to me, because in my mind the worship experience was a tool to deliver "salvation to the lost." Each component of our worship service had to be powerful, flawless, and moving so that we could use these elements to stir people's emotions. Hopefully their response to our music would urge them to engage in "a relationship with Jesus." Ideally, the "lost souls" in our midst would encounter the "Holy Spirit" during our worship tunes or after one of our elaborate productions. This would initiate the beginning of the "discipleship process."

In the "discipleship process" we hoped that an encounter with "The Spirit" would spur visitors to officially become "Christians" by reciting the prewritten magical prayer stuffed in their weekly bulletins. After reading the "prayer for salvation," these new "Christians" would be taught to pray in our church's specialized classes. Preferably, they would even speak in "tongues" over time. They would join a small group, and the culmination of all of these steps meant that they would eventually lose their desire to drink, smoke, do drugs, have premarital sex, be gay, or vote Democrat. If they "stumbled" into any of their "old ways," they would have to get "saved again."

The most important step for our new members becoming good "Christians" was that they would begin to tithe a sizable portion of their annual income. Starting at 10 percent.

———◆ ┃━━━

I can imagine that as people read this story, they are ruminating about a similar church in their area code that fits this exact description. I guarantee that a massive hall of theatrics meant to entertain those who identify as Christian is somewhere in your general vicinity. This model is notorious for being satiated with thieves and hypocrites.

The word "hypocrite" in the New Testament is derived from the Koine Greek word *hypokrites*. This word captures a much broader definition than a sanctimonious adherent. The word literally means "one who acts." It would seem that when this word is used in the Scriptures, it describes those who actually engage in religious stage-craft. The dominance of megachurch culture in America would indicate that both atheists and agnostics have been accurate when they assume that the Church is a harbor for "hypocrites."

To quote Reggie McNeal, "We have 'Six Flags Over Jesus' in every city of the United States."

This method of "doing church" has become prevalent in the United States for one simple reason. It works. The most attended churches in the U.S. have a strikingly similar approach to this worship style while also attracting a large audience of young adults as their regular attendees. Yet, they also have the same irrational theological and scientific views as older and more traditional evangelical communities.

Churches like this one are not just hazardous because of the doctrines they edify. Plenty of perishing traditional churches teach an identical philosophy, but their days are numbered. Megachurches, and conservative "hip churches," are dangerous because of the massive numbers they attract to absorb that teaching. Evangelicals are adept at wielding cultural relevance to sow a destructive influence.

I have seen it.

Hell, I've done it.

It is a truly brilliant tactic. Evil, but brilliant nonetheless.

Modern fundamentalists have used an open approach to methodology to "evangelize" people even though their theology remains ignorant, uneducated, and closed-minded.

Obviously, the epidemic of the American megachurch is a disease, but in their parishioners' defense, many Americans are unaware of a theological alternative outside of Southern Baptist or charismatic Pentecostal interpretations of the Bible. Both of which happen to be the prevailing denominations in our culture, and, unfortunately, both sects are often intolerant and detrimental. This is why our ability as progressive Christians to oppose these spaces is paramount.

Take me for example:

When I found my current denomination, the Disciples of Christ (DOC), I was new to liberal/progressive ideas, and I had only been exposed to these alternative schools of thought by literature. So I began calling the agents of writers that inspired me.

Eventually I got a call back from one of my favorite progressive Christian authors, Brian McLaren. After I recovered from the shock of being on the phone with one of my idols, Brian recommended the Disciples of Christ to me. I had never heard of the denomination before Brian McLaren recommended them as a viable option. Being from the Bible Belt, I had never seen a "progressive church" before, nor was I even aware that an entire network of folks who are as crazy as I am even existed. I assumed that in my rural city, I was alone in my faith journey to flee Christian conservatism. Yet, Brian explained to me that there were many denominations that shared my views beyond the Disciples of Christ.

I was shocked! Where had they been for the last century?

We have a saying in the Disciples that we are the best-kept secret in American Christianity. I wholly agree with that assessment, but I also am sick and damn tired of being a secret when evangelicals claiming to be the gatekeepers of Christ's teachings are succeeding in their mission of being the most prominent voices of Christendom in America.

In spite of this annoyance, and because of the unintentional underground nature of my denomination, part of me is grateful that my journey began in evangelical spaces. Because as amazing as the mainline progressive approach is to hermeneutics and homiletics, we largely are ineffective in tangibly reaching a younger audience in comparison to our evangelical counterparts.

The "mainline decline" is a descriptor of the plummeting attendance within progressive denominations. This recession has been in full effect for over forty years. If you think about it, you know this is a real problem because the "mainline decline" has existed long enough to acquire a rhyming label. By comparison, conservative megachurches are not dying. Disturbingly, many are thriving.

I hypothesize that this success of the megachurch is partially due to the fact that it has never had sufficient opposition in Christendom.

Why?

Because we progressives have the opposite problem in our worship spaces compared to evangelicalism. We progressives are flexible in examining theological views, but we are absolute in our commitment to nurturing tradition. Much of which is meaningless at best and triggering at worst for the average young adult in today's society. Most millennials find little value in robes, altars, creeds, temples, and songs written 150 years ago. While the evangelical church has yet to accept the indisputable reality of scientific truths such as evolution. As a whole, those of us in the progressive mainline have yet to evolve in our approach to worship.

This is tragic. Some of the finest sermons I have heard in my career have been found in the halls of high liturgy. Yet for the most part, young people are not attracted to these spaces.

We progressives can no longer allow ourselves to remain tone deaf to the language and culture of our nation's future leaders, and we must accept that the moment we stop being relevant is the moment that the progressive church can no longer transcend time and endure as a positive influence in the future.

So what then?

Do we pursue a model that resembles the "Six Flags over Jesus" blueprint?

No!

HELL NO!

I believe that what we need to do as progressive Christians is far more challenging than mimicking the success of our opposition. We must innovate. We must explore methodology that never has been attempted in American churches that appeals to a younger demographic and that simultaneously embodies the radical politically subversive movement of the early church.

Now, if we progressives do decide to evolve in our liturgical approach, there is another dilemma.

Evangelicals beat us to the punch.

They dumped their temples for concert halls years ago. The best of them can put on a U2-esque concert every weekend. I know, because we did. These venues come fully equipped with a children's area as entertaining as an arcade and a café with cold brew just as acrid as Starbucks. The poor quality of coffee alone means that we progressives do not want to resemble these spaces.

It is safe to say that many in the Christian Left face the dilemma of letting go of our spiritual style in order to seek relevance. In so doing, we often fear that in our pursuit of innovation we're modeling our worship after evangelicals, but we cannot let this stop us. We can make our services attractive, without becoming an attraction. If we continue to refuse the pursuit of relevance, it ensures that the radical teachings of Christ will lose its ability to transcend time. Progressive Christians must ask ourselves if we want to cling to tradition more than we want the Gospel to be solely preached from evangelical pulpits and used for their harmful agenda. For if we do not modify this dynamic in the next decade, that could be the future of American Christianity.

So what do we do? Are we are at a crossroads? (#punny)

Parroting megachurches would not be innovation. It would be appropriation, and that is not what needs to happen for the mainline to experience growth.

Why?

The current success of the megachurch ultimately will dwindle. Traditional worship in progressive cathedrals and postmodern worship within evangelical worship halls are literally the same format as one another, just different styles. Both spaces were built under the theological premise that God desires to reside in large, complex structures. Both have spent ungodly amounts of wealth to construct. Both require large numbers of tithing congregants to sustain themselves. Both focus much of their clergy's attention in creating a weekly production rather than producing disciples. Both are properties that are a pain in the ass to maintain, and, lastly, the world is frankly growing sick of both venues.

So we have to advance beyond both spaces.

Besides, based on scriptural descriptions of God's qualities, the God of the Bible would be disgusted by now with both the megachurch, and the cathedral. One simply needs to look to the text to accept this axiom.

Think about it:

The tower of Babel = Destroyed

Tables of the Temple = Flipped

The Temple Veil = Torn

We keep building more elaborate and expensive religious facilities and services, but God keeps tearing that shit down. It is as if the

Divine has been telling us that our religious spaces and artifacts were never the point. I dare say that if Jesus were here today, that this passionate Rabbi would overturn altars in both settings. After all, it is not like the God depicted in the Scriptures had much appreciation for grand architecture.

In short, the horse of Christendom is symbolically dead, but even an electric guitar, faux hawk, skinny jeans, an iPad, and a concert hall won't make it stink any less.

By the time midnight rolled around, I entered my van exhausted from a long night's rehearsal. I turned on some Christian rock and drove out of the parking lot and toward the street. I had been employed by this church for over a year, and I still hadn't noticed the three trailer parks surrounding our church property, nor had I asked why we weren't doing anything to serve some of the poorest families in the county that lived in those RVs.

"Lord, thank you for this night," I said, neglecting to glance at the tattered modular domiciles in every cardinal direction surrounding our facility.

"I could feel your Holy Spirit among us," I arrogantly proclaimed in reverent gratitude, as I finished my prayer.

In case you are curious about the outcome of our production of Jesus walking on water, it was quite impressive to our congregation. Tears were shed that day. Both as an emotional response from folks witnessing our dramatization and perhaps also from a single parent residing in the trailer park behind our sanctuary sobbing over a pink eviction notice in their hands, because they couldn't raise five children on minimum wage.

SCALES

"Okay, so here is the plan. I think I'm going to head your way around 4:00 a.m. on Tuesday. I will drive straight through the morning. I should get there just in time for lunch. I will pick you up, and we will go downtown to get some legit Cajun cookin'! Love ya. See ya soon, oh, and by the way, first round is on you," I said jokingly just before hanging up.

I was delighted to finally leave the confines of the Low Country and see the world.

My destination?

New Orleans!

I was twenty-one years old, and I had never been more than thirty miles away from the town in which I was raised. Though my traveling had been severely limited, remaining close to my stomping grounds was a personal decision based in insecurity.

The acute isolationism of many southern conservatives is a byproduct of fear-based propaganda. There is so much terror surrounding the concept of the "other" and frightening "liberal ideals" that many rural southerners often prefer seclusion. They only venture outside of their hometowns or explore what is going on in our government by watching FOX "News." Then this clearly twisted and biased media outlet shares perspectives from folks like Sean Hannity and Tucker Carlson, which ultimately causes these frightened Republican viewers to remain quarantined in their familiar world. No matter how small that world may be.

Luckily for me, this trip wasn't too far outside of my comfort zone. I only was going a few states over to Louisiana. Even if this particular journey had been to Portland, Oregon (the cultural equivalent to Mordor in the eyes of fundamentalists), I would have sojourned without question because the person I had just spoken with on the phone was my best friend Sean.

Sean is like the twin sibling I never had. We initially connected at a Friday night collegiate Bible Study for young adults. The study was an ecumenical space stationed in a humble room that seated around fifty people. It was relatively successful for an eclectic gathering of evangelicals. Its success was by virtue of its stylistic approach. Back then, one of the most edgy and attractive venues a Christian organization could emulate was a coffee shop. These spaces flourished no matter how shitty the quality of their coffee, and, oh, was our coffee shitty.

We cultivated this space together with a frugal budget. We stocked it with used couches and cheap metal folding chairs, and we served the finest premium Piggly Wiggly coffee in off-brand styrofoam cups.

Every Friday night, Christians eighteen to twenty-nine years of age from varying local churches would gather, worship, study scripture, and share life with one another. This experience has remained an inspiration when I am shaping worship spaces for the twenty-first century. Even though our collective theology was terribly misguided, our modern methodology of doing life together was effective and genuinely meaningful.

I had been in and out of this ministry as a volunteer for some time because of my conflicting work schedule. One night I was asked to act as a substitute for the musical portion of the service. That is where Sean and I were first introduced.

Sean volunteered in the sound booth that night. This required me to make a good impression with Sean, because any career musician will tell you that if you want a high quality show then the happiest person in your circumference better be the audio engineer. Sound technicians can hit the "suck button" at a moment's notice if they choose.

I am fairly certain that Sean saw precisely through my attempts to brown nose, but regardless of this the worship went fairly well. After the musical portion of the night was over, rather than mingling with folks whom I barely knew, I did what all extreme introverts do. I hid in the back, and I was in luck because a sound booth is a socially anxious soul's dream come true. My fear of conversing with total strangers is how Sean and I became better acquainted. Sean was hiding in the back as well. I introduced myself and we attempted to have a dialogue. To my surprise, we shared an instant connection over our love of high calorie foods, comic books, fictional fantasy literature, sci-fi television, and Xbox games. Sean and I would continue to grow closer as time passed. So close, actually, that about a year after being introduced, Sean's encouragement would be solely responsible for solidifying my career in ministry.

I was still employed by the megachurch, and though my skills were adequate, something unexplainable was causing a major lack of fulfillment in my career. Where once my ambitions in ministry were lucid, they had begun to feel fuzzy and distant. Every Sunday, people were interacting positively with our music, and it appeared that people were experiencing a force greater than themselves. At every service, dozens of people would leave the altar with tears in their eyes as we played our love songs to Jesus, and every Sunday, I left feeling empty as if my soul was famished. What had once brought a sense of intimacy with my Creator and given me a sense of purpose was now filled with irritability, uncertainty, and the drudgery of church politics.

Every damn week there was an unavoidable struggle with older white congregants. It never failed that despite massive approval from most of our church members, complaints from a handful of wealthy baby boomers about our modern musical style would emerge the following week. This infuriated our entire music team. The protests from these parishioners made absolutely no sense. It is not like we suddenly changed our style or target demographic over-night. A rock concert is what we had always been. There were stage lights, projectors, and a drum set on a six-foot pedestal. They knew what kind of church that they were getting into when they walked in the door, and their attempts to change our style were consistently obnoxious and forever growing in intensity. These criticisms didn't bother me. Being forced to coddle these privileged snobs is what truly irked me.

I could handle the insignificant number of grievances, but I loathed being forced to submit to the entitled attitude of these moneybags because they "preferred church the old way." Were it anyone else grumbling, our church leadership would not give two shits, but because the source of disgruntlement emerged from the wealth-iest members of the church and possibly the entire city, we had been instructed to compromise. Even if it meant losing hundreds of other members, we were forced into submission. Because of this bureaucratic bullshit, it was becoming increasingly difficult to remain silent, and I was practically prepared to tell the oligarchs exactly how I felt. Consequences be damned.

But as frustratingly impossible as it was to please those conservative, white, and wealthy baby boomers, it was not my only source of irritation. There also was my growing discontent for the theatrics of it all. Rehearsing when band members would lift our hands in response to "The Holy Spirit" to seem "more worshipful" and plan-ning when we would perform stanzas of these songs on our knees to display "submission to the Spirit" felt like a betrayal of any possibil-ity for a genuine encounter with the Divine. There was no instance of "anointing" felt by our congregation that wasn't initiated by injecting our prefabricated charismatic Christian expressions.

One day after weeks of complaining about my career to my best friend, Sean offered me a gift that saved my ministry. We met together for lunch, and I was venting heavily in the middle of another whining session.

"Maybe I should be done with church. I am still young and I have time to pursue something else. Maybe this whole idea of a ministerial 'calling' was self-induced. I am obviously not cut out for this kind of employment," I groaned.

"Christopher, come on! Get it together! Look, you sound defeated. Have you ever thought that the environment that is frustrating you is what needs to change, not your involvement with it? Maybe that is what you are called to do?" Sean proposed.

"I dunno if I have the patience or desire to keep wearing this mask though. It's all horse shit anyway," I mumbled, staring at the floor.

That's when Sean reached into a book bag sitting on a nearby table and pulled out *Velvet Elvis* by Rob Bell, and *Blue Like Jazz* by Donald Miller.

"Give these a read. A lot of topics that you and I have been talking about lately are mentioned in these books. Especially the elements of church that you have been critical of," Sean said. "I don't believe that you are alone in these observations. These books may guide you. They might not. I don't have a crystal ball, but maybe just knowing that you are not alone will give you some encouragement to keep pressing onward," Sean said while placing a hand on my shoulder.

I think those of us familiar with these two works of Christian literature can acknowledge that neither book is "that progressive" by modern standards, but the present definition of "progressive" is a bad metric. According to my pastors back then, I might as well have been reading a copy of *The Communist Manifesto*. *So* I took both books hesitantly because of the controversy from fundamentalists that was surrounding these two authors.

Shockingly, Sean was right. These were life-changing works.

The theological views were so counter to the points I had always heard from the pulpit. Yet, these two publications struck me not as heretical, but as hidden truths. It was the first time I had observed anything regarding spirituality that gripped me. Truly gripped me. I could not put either of these bestsellers down. The only sensation I could compare reading them to was like reading *A Song of Ice and Fire* for the first time (*Game of Thrones* for the lay nerds), or like enjoying the Harry Potter series in the early 2000s before the books were made into films.

It was as if Rob and Don had been simultaneously sent to me by divine appointment to provide relief from my struggle. That is a self-absorbed notion to be sure, but these two literary sources were exactly what I needed at this moment of my life.

I owe my career and every positive impact I will ever have in ministry to Don, Rob, and especially Sean. Without the encouragement I received from these three, I would have surrendered to conformity in corporate America years ago.

That was quite a rabbit trail wasn't it? Back to the story.

Months before the phone call I described in the opening of this chapter, Sean had decided to move to New Orleans because Sean had gotten engaged to our friend Kristen. Kristen's family was moving to Louisiana, and neither Kristen nor Sean were excited about the complexities of a possible long-distance relationship. So, with very little notice, Sean packed up all of their personal belongings into a beat-up pickup truck and relocated to NOLA. Despite our promise to remain in contact, I was terrified that this venture would be the end of our friendship.

My fears soon were proven to be baseless. During this season I learned that time, and distance, cannot change the bonds of true kinship, because Sean and I continued to communicate frequently despite our differing geographic locations.

Months after Sean relocated to The Big Easy, Sean made the decision to enlist in the United States Coast Guard. This would require basic training for two months, and during that time, Kristen had nowhere to stay. They called to ask if Kristen could live with me back on the East Coast until Sean's basic training was complete. I considered Kristen to be family as well, so of course the answer was "yes." After I agreed to let Kristen stay with me for a time, Sean explained that this temporary arrangement also called for someone to help drive their belongings back east to be placed in storage.

That was the reason for our phone call.

The deal was that if I would make the journey, and if I would offer assistance in bringing their belongings back East, they would reimburse my gas, provide the cost of my Cajun food/craft beer intake, and supply my lodging while I was in New Orleans.

I had recently purchased a Toyota Prius, so a six-hour drive hardly would disrupt my checking account. Besides, to my regret I had never been to New Orleans. As a music lover and Cajun food connoisseur, the lack of a Big Easy experience would no longer do.

Little did I know that this trip would be the first of many steps on a pilgrimage toward progressive Christianity.

Hurricane Katrina had made landfall the year before my inaugural visit. The damage from the tempest's aftermath was still visible. As I approached Mississippi and Louisiana, I was aghast with how quickly climate crisis can obliterate a landscape. FEMA trailers riddled the horizon for miles, and even though months had passed since this horrific storm struck, there was still wreckage scattered throughout the marshlands and decorating the swamps.

My pastor preached that God created this Category 5 hurricane to punish the citizens of New Orleans. Funny, the last thing I saw in the conclusion of Katrina was God's fingerprint. How could an "all loving God" manifest something so destructive and cruel to slaughter hundreds and still be considered to be a good God by anyone?

I arrived in the city limits of New Orleans around noon, and greeted my friend whom I hadn't seen in months with a solid embrace. After dropping my things at Sean's mobile home, we immediately set off for downtown.

Even in the wake of Katrina, New Orleans was everything I had hoped it would be and so much more.

The streets were bursting with musicians. Artists playing dilapidated musical instruments while still managing to make them sound heavenly could be heard for blocks. There were dozens of singers on every corner with better vocal abilities than most professionals I had heard in concert venues. Dancers erupted through the sidewalks and were breathtaking to behold. They leaped and moved with featherlike grace on street corners. Each of them attracting massive crowds to gather around them.

This city was magical.

Literally, there was magic.

Street magicians performed impossible illusions that still have me baffled to this day. Their craft dazzled tourists and generated buckets of tips. It was clear that every block pulsed with true talent in New Orleans.

We continued to walk down the street and absorb all the amazing culture that is New Orleans. The artists lined the streets with their work. The jewelers displayed their sparkling handmade products for sale. There were bars placed every three to five commercial spaces downtown. Each taproom dripped in Creole charm, and to my delight, each of them served their beer in to-go cups.

Before lunch, we decided to have an obligatory visit to the eerie local voodoo shops. As a proper evangelical, I initially objected to visiting such places, but I am glad I was persuaded. Candles with crushed herbs, arcane books, cracked skulls, and dark tapestries were on display, sending chills down my spine as I passed them. Thinking back, I would have been embarrassed to be with me. I was the stereotypical charismatic who was rebuking demonic spirits under my breath as I viewed all of their Gothic wares. Yet even those creepy aesthetics were somehow vibrant and beautiful.

The only thing more delicious than the sounds and decorum of New Orleans is the flavor. I had never heard of their French fried pillowy clouds called *beignets* before, and if you have never enjoyed them in New Orleans, I dare say that you still do not comprehend what real beignets are. We devoured these heavenly pastries with a cup of fresh chicory coffee at Cafe du Monde, and as we were chatting we noticed that adjacent to our table a movie was being filmed. As a rural southerner, I was overwhelmed with the culture of this incredible city.

We finished our coffee and continued to explore the French Quarter. All the while I continued to drop pieces of my soul down the streets of this majestic metropolis. We wandered around for a few hours, stopping every few blocks to enjoy a craft beer, and catch up with one another. Conversation becomes less burdensome when you stop every three to four bars for an additional Abita brew.

Eventually in our wanderings, the aroma of Cajun cuisine stoked our appetite. So Sean and I decided to visit a local delicatessen. This diner could give patrons a coronary just by smelling the food that was being prepared. It was superb. We ate our fill of exquisite alligator etouffée, decadent crawfish gumbo, spicy red beans and rice, and crispy shrimp po' boys.

After exiting the restaurant, we turned onto Bourbon Street with every intent of taking in more sites. We each had another beer in hand and Sean had our leftovers in tow. (If I am being completely transparent, they were only Sean's leftovers. My meal wasn't on my plate for long after it was handed to me.)

We were in mid-sentence turning the corner when a teenager by the name of Eli approached us riding a rusted bicycle. Eli was young with a stubble beard, tiny frame, and long blond dreadlocks. Eli's attire was filthy, and our new acquaintance appeared to be malnourished and weakened.

Curiously, I have forgotten many faces in the memories of my youth, but not this one. Eli is a photograph forever sketched in my subconscious.

Eli announced innocent intentions and made a loud, awkward introduction immediately upon approaching us.

"Geaux Tigers! Hey y'all, I am not going to ask you for any money, but I haven't eaten in three days. Could I just have those leftovers? I am sorry to ask, but I am starving," Eli pleaded, desperately.

Sean immediately presented the box of the remaining Cajun sustenance. As the food changed hands, I had a sudden realization of how sheltered my life had been up until this moment. I had never met someone experiencing homelessness.

Not once.

Sure, I had known people who were living in poverty. I, myself, was certainly no stranger to it. Poverty and I were old friends, but in my twenty-two years, I had never met someone who did not have an actual warm bed to return to at the end of the day.

I experienced a series of blended emotions about this encounter. I concurrently felt naive, obligated, and guilty. Sensing that I had to offer something meaningful to aid Eli, I reached for my wallet longing to alleviate this teenager's suffering and presented a twenty-dollar bill.

Like a proper conservative Christian, I could not provide this young stranger funds in good conscience without an obligatory "Jesus loves you." When the words passed from my teeth and into Eli's ears, I expected to witness gratitude on my new friend's face. Maybe even hope. Instead, I saw disbelief. Eli's large grayish blue eyes began to water.

"Are you serious? No one helps anyone here. Especially Christians," uttered Eli.

In an instant, Eli had immediately amplified the lens through which I viewed this city. Mass suffering had escaped my initial observation of this town.

Isn't it interesting how one person's paradise can become another's prison? One's source of inspiration can be another's detriment, and one's alternative truth can augment our perception of reality?

I began to see NOLA in a completely different light. This city, like many others in our nation, had a carrot for its tourists, but a stick for its poorest residents. Its entire existence was dependent on privileged white tourists spending tremendous amounts of money in exchange for their drinks, food, trinkets, and souvenirs. Until this moment, I completely missed the culture of desperation swallowing locals just like Eli. There were so many residents living in poverty and homelessness who had been invisible to me.

Where once I had expressed adoration in exploring this city, now I was also experiencing grief for those trapped on its streets. There were churches downtown whose architecture that I admired just a few hours prior to this chance conversation, but after talking with Eli, I noticed metal bars on the windows of those same elaborate temples. It is amazing to think of the dichotomy between how I viewed this city prior to, and preceding, this encounter. Where once there was beauty, cathedrals, creativity, history, and art, post-Eli there would only be schemes, spiritual prisons, disgust, grief, and hypocrisy. These vile things had been before my eyes the whole time, but it took me seeing the perspective of a homeless person to realize how blind I always had been.

Storefront churches located in downtown with locked commercial spaces had signs that read, "Ring Buzzer to Schedule a Meeting With Clergy." Another had a plaque that stated, "Shoes Required" right on their front door.

How could this be? How could these temples be so blind to their willful indifference? How could Christians witness abject poverty on a daily basis, and remain docile with no initiatives to end this localized injustice?

It was at this point in my zealous indignation that the reality of my blatant hypocrisy smacked me in the face.

As I mentioned in the previous chapter, social injustice in every possible direction surrounded the venue of my church back home, and despite having intimate knowledge of our annual budget (which was quite large), I never had questioned why we had not attempted to create any sort of communal program to assist struggling neighbors in our immediate vicinity. My focus in creating a powerful worship service had blinded me to opportunities in servitude of the downtrodden who were in proximity to our sanctuary doors.

I, too, was guilty of neglect in the first degree.

I started leaving different pieces of my heart on the streets of New Orleans that afternoon. Only this time, the pieces were in shards. Those fragmented remains are still buried in NOLA. While a myriad of my emotions were paced over historic cobblestone, somewhere along those famous brick sidewalks lay the scales that fell from my eyes.

Like the apostle Paul (aka Saul), I never personally witnessed the living Jesus that I claim to follow. Like Saul, I once hatefully persecuted people in the name of a God that the Scriptures define as being constructed of love itself. Like Saul, I had failed to see the irony of my ways. I perpetuated suffering by endorsing statues of belief that either deemed certain peoples unworthy of God's love or habitually ignored opportunities that were wholesome and worthwhile. Fortunately for me, and for Saul, there was an awakening.

Paul (the artist formerly known as Saul) had a transformation that can be found in the ninth chapter of the book of Acts:

Saul fell to the ground and heard a voice saying, "Saul, Saul, why do you persecute me?" Saul asked, "Who are you, Lord?" The reply came, "I am Jesus, whom you are persecuting. But get up and enter the city, and you will be told what you are to do." The people who were traveling with Saul stood speechless because they heard the voice but saw no one. Saul got up from the ground, and though their eyes were open, but they could see nothing; so they led Saul by the hand and brought them into Damascus. For three days Saul was without sight, and neither ate nor drank.

Now there was a disciple in Damascus named Ananias. The Lord said in a vision, "Ananias." They answered, "Here I am, Lord." The Lord said to them, "Get up and go to the street called Straight, and at the house of Judas look for a citizen of Tarsus named Saul. At this moment Saul is praying, and has seen in a vision that someone named Ananias will come in and lay their hands on Saul so that they might regain sight." But Ananias answered, "Lord, I have heard from many about this person, how much evil have they done to your saints in Jerusalem; and here Saul has authority from the chief priests to bind all who invoke your name." But the Lord said, "Go, for Saul is an instrument whom I have chosen to bring my name before Gentiles and Rulers and before the people of Israel; I myself will show Saul how much they must suffer for the sake of my name." So Ananias went and entered the house. Ananias laid his hands on Saul and said, "Saul, the Lord Jesus, who appeared to you on your way here, has sent me so that you may regain your sight and be filled with the Holy Spirit." And immediately something like scales fell from Saul's eyes, and sight was restored. Then Saul got up and was baptized.

Before this encounter with Eli on the streets of The Big Easy, I saw a magical city being reformed. A city that many evangelicals disgustingly believed was left in ruins because of God's judgement on homosexuality. I shamefully regret that, at this time, I felt this way too. I distinctly recall the sermon in which my pastor utilized the imagery of Noah and the flood as a metaphor for Katrina and its victims. Even though we saw the world through this harsh lens, we somehow believed that we were being gracious. We even sent money to mission workers to rebuild what remained of this "sinful city," as long as these missionaries bestowed our evangelical beliefs in that community as well. Our seemingly "unconditional love" was only offered with conditional reassurance.

When I read this story of Saul's transformation, it reminds me that many evangelicals are on their own modern-day mission to Damascus. Like Saul, fundamentalists are on a crusade to persecute innocents. Like Saul, their dangerous intent is clouded. They believe their motives are pure, but their cultural footprint indicates that their pilgrimage for righteousness is leading to the destruction of innocents. In this knowledge, if we make an honest assessment of the essence of western Christianity, then it is obvious that the God of the Bible has been plagued with identity theft.

The Church's intolerance of LGBTQ folks, willful ignorance regarding climate change, consistent refusal to let women lead, denying those who identify as women the right to choose what IS right for their own bodies, etc.

All of these crimes are indicative of a present-day evangelical crusade.

A crusade for THEIR God, a crusade for THEIR values, and a crusade that the historical Jesus certainly would have opposed.

Because of this, it is easy to become infuriated with the hatred of self-identified Christians who are hateful, but in the midst of our rage, there remains hope. That hope is clearly written in the pages of my own testimony.

Like Saul, I was once blinded by religion, but during my tenure as a religious extremist, I somehow managed to discover a better way. For those reading this who have all but given up on conservative Christians and the possibility of them ever transcending from the pit of their malevolence, I wish to offer you a spark of optimism. Even those who are utterly lost and wholly devoted to vile rhetoric can change. I know, because I did, and so did Saul.

But it will take the efforts of many gallant leaders who are willing to rescue conservatives from their darkness. It will take many chaplains of transformation.

Agents of change just like Ananias in the book of Acts.

Notice that it is Ananias' participation that is necessary in removing the scales from Saul's eyes. Not God's. Ananias' willingness was vital in the chronicle of Saul's transformation. Ananias was obedient and played a vital role that restored this blind warmonger knowing full well that persecution was a possible outcome.

Because of this, I believe that the moral hero in this story in Acts is not Saul.

It isn't God.

It is a fearful follower named Ananias.

Plenty of early Christians would have experienced dread similar to Ananias if they were in the same situation. Ananias would have been a target of this zealot named Saul. Saul was a persecutor of the early church and as a member of the early church, Ananias knew Saul's reputation. If Saul had not experienced a dilemma of sight and met Ananias under differing circumstances, then Saul would have had our hero stoned to death for blasphemy. This is why Ananias questioned God about using someone as vicious as Saul to lead the church. The notion of Saul being able to transcend extremism would have been tough for anyone to accept. Yet, this humble servant was brave enough to eventually see that the potential for Paul was within Saul.

That's what I love about the Scriptures. Those labeled "heretics" by institution are often portrayed as the heroes.

Looking back on my own life, I am sure that others felt a similar hesitation about my ability to change as well. I was a sexist, racist, homophobic piece of shit. Many people would have made that assessment accurately and labeled me accordingly. Thankfully I had many precious and painful encounters that forced me to realize that my eyes were clouded, and had been for quite some time. Just like Saul.

Unlike Saul, my complete healing was not instantaneous. I would not truly recognize my need for redemption until years later, but I was blessed to have had many of my own "Ananiases" of sorts at different points of my life who reached out to me and guided my steps. Eli was one of them.

As time passed, my spiritual teachers provided relief that came in the form of firm words of rebuke, but these Ananiases refused to abandon me to execration. They saw me not only as a victimizer, but as a victim as well. To them I was a prisoner of a volatile religion that bound me in misery. In their minds I was a person with potential that endured brainwashing, gaslighting, and manipulation by a religious system that used my eagerness to serve God in order to to advance a filthy agenda.

Though I claimed to be a Christ follower, I did not fully comprehend that contextual Christianity was intended to shatter our religious chains, not facilitate dogmatic entrapment. These many Ananiases helped me learn the nature of my moral blindness. Thank God for the Ananias in Saul's story, and my own. For without them I would still be lost, and the early church would have lost a prominent figure that would be renamed Paul.

I believe that this same capacity for goodness resides in every fundamentalist who is living in a present darkness.

The God of both testaments beckons the victimized to firmly call out their victimizer while simultaneously discouraging reciprocation of enmity. The Scriptures dares us to speak the potential for positivity over extremists in the midst of their evildoing. This implies that we change this world not by hurting those who hurt, not by hurling violence at the vile, and not by abandoning those who make refuge necessary, but by reconstructing the calloused hearts of our adversaries with words of fierce truth spoken bravely in love.

Love never wields hatred, but in the face of hate love must be louder.

We are reminded here that change is possible if we refuse to give up on those who are lost to unjust procedures of intolerance. We call out their missteps boldly. We guide them as they fumble away from the void. We lead them in their blindness with words of education. We instruct with sharp words of truth about their character flaws. Most importantly, we provide a living example counter to the unethical ethos of colonization and Americanized Christianity.

Until recently, I have been struggling with whether or not I would prefer to be labeled a "Christian." My reasoning for this internal debate was that this moniker has been perverted in order to inflict some pretty horrific shit throughout history.

I have recently decided that this course of action (though tempting) is far too easy. By surrendering the label of "Christian" to conservatives who look nothing like Christ, we remove our responsibility to correct their cultural impacts that are a direct result of their ethical blindness.

If this story found in the book of Acts is any sort of symbolic blueprint for everyday praxis, then it should encourage us to approach institutional opposition, demand that justice be done, and declare that despite our enemy's present identity, there remains the possibility for righteousness, atonement, repentance, and restoration.

The social activist Dorothy Day said it best: *"The Church may be a whore at times, but the Church is still my mother."*

Without Ananias, you only ever had Saul, and a similar challenge of Saul's conversion is before the progressive wing of the Church today. The possibility regarding The Christian Left's collective abandonment of the term "Christian" is simply not in the cards. If these lessons extracted from Acts have any sort of bearing on this matter, this should not be an option.

According to the story of Saul and Ananias, metaphorically gifting sight to morally blind assholes who hijack the faith for dangerous initiatives is a burden that all Christ followers must bear, and in America it is a mandate that long has been forgotten.

As we said goodbye to this young stranger who exposed my spiritual depravity, the atmosphere adjusted accordingly with my inner turmoil. We turned down the next street, and the smell of precipitation was crisp in the air. Before our eyes, the sky blackened, and within seconds a torrential southern downpour exploded over the French Quarter. Storm drains flooded within minutes as we scurried through ankle-deep rain puddles on the long hike back to my Toyota Prius.

We jumped in the car, and as I started the hybrid engine, I remember seeing a pink slip on my window. As I am writing this, I am reminded that I may still have an unpaid parking ticket in New Orleans from thirteen years ago, but I digress.

We decided to head back to Sean's trailer and rendezvous with Kristen so we could begin preparations for the journey back to the Low Country. The next day as we left the city limits, I meditated about all that had occurred on this expedition. I have never been so conflicted about a city in my life. With each mile away from this art-filled mecca that was both arbiter of life and harbinger of my own inner demons, I was more grateful to have laid my dreams, hopes, and ambitions, corrupted by religiosity, to rest on the historic brick paths of New Orleans.

GOSPELS

I was lounging on the sanctuary floor staring up at the rack-mounted lights illuminating our darkened stage. I lay motionless with my gaze locked on the spot light that brightened my official position as the worship leader.

I was terribly conflicted, dreading the Sunday service.

Since I had returned from New Orleans, I had become numb to all tasks surrounding my employment. This chapel was nothing more than a house of cinematics, and as time passed, I realized that my occupation was merely intended to be a tool of performance. This was a concert, nothing more, and it was no longer a production that I desired to be a part of.

After my ordeal in Louisiana, I shared multiple ideas with our church board to create service programs that would benefit our city's poorest residents. Our senior "pastor" shut down every concept without exception and dismissed any possibility of our church aiding the community. I was told that benevolence was not part of our job description, and I needed to focus on feeding people "The Word of God," not daydreaming about a food pantry that could actually feed them. The authorities of this congregation made it clear that I was hired to play their music, submit to their every decision, and keep my opinions to myself. But leading their high quality renditions of subpar U2-esque Jesus rock no longer had the same appeal. What once brought pleasure, and even a sense of purpose, now had offered nothing but regret, and possibly acid reflux.

I rested on the dark gray industrial carpet recalling how I felt before my trip to NOLA. I could remember how it once seemed as if

God's presence was resting in the midst of our sanctuary. Now, I felt duped as if I had been sucked into a cult.

Looking back, it WAS a cult.

Our stage, lighting, speakers, HD projectors, and our expensive instruments had become beacons of our church's poor stewardship of morality. The cost of our spectacular equipment became equations in my brain that represented funds that were poorly managed. That money could have been allocated to nourishing the hungry right outside our door, rather than feeding emotional addicts their weekly dose of tear-inducing ballads to Jesus.

I sat up with a deep sigh, opened my computer, and began the task of arranging songs for Sunday's service, a task that previously was gratifying for me. On the screen I reviewed the spiritual poetry wrapped in repetitive four-chord progressions. These songs were now hollow, and it was hard to believe that they had been a source of inspiration just months prior. Worship lyrics and hymns were now anthems of my own depravity.

As I was glancing at my MacBook with eyes half-awake and my mind half-focused on the task at hand, a shadowy figure entered from the back of the sanctum. This enigmatic silhouette appeared to be calling out for my attention.

This happening was quite surprising because I had presumed that our sanctuary doors were locked. I removed my BOSE headphones that were blasting Hillsong's latest album from my iPod and approached my unexpected visitor.

"Are you the pastor, and is that your sports car outside?" my unexpected guest inquired curiously with a heavy southern twang.

"No, I am not, and I wish that car belonged to me. It does belong to the pastor, though, but all of our senior ministers are currently in a prayer meeting. I am a minister of music here. Can I help you?" I replied timidly, not because this individual appeared threatening, but because I have always been painfully shy.

This random stranger was conceivably around my age, and as I got closer to the figure I noticed the details of tattered and filthy attire. In the foyer I spied another petite young person wearing a ripped Care Bear T-shirt with long unkempt hair thrown up carelessly in a lackadaisical ponytail standing with a toddler on one hip and an infant on the other.

"My name is Jason and this is Krystal. Our pickup ran out of gas so I pushed it into y'alls' lot. Our truck is really old and guzzles fuel. Unfortunately, the gas gauge is broken too. We have been driving all day, stopping every couple of hours for gas. Well, to make a long story short, I must have done the numbers wrong at the last stop. I thought I had enough to make it to the gas station a couple exits down the road. Apparently math isn't my forté. Anyway, I have money for gas, but not enough for gas cans to bring the fuel back. I was wondering if you all had a couple lying around here that I could borrow? I could walk to the gas station and bring 'em right back if that's okay?" asked Jason.

"Fine by me," I said, as I made a silly face to the shy kids hiding their eyes in the armpits of the Care Bear T-shirt.

"Would it be okay if my kids could wait here inside and out of this heat?" Jason asked.

I saw the sweaty faces of the two tiny children wearing denim over-alls and no undershirts. How could I say no?

I was uncertain about the policy for allowing the general public into our worship hall, but I could not turn away this couple. Being trapped outdoors without an AC in the middle of a Low Country summer, and having every drop of hemoglobin drained by sand gnats, yellow flies, and mosquitos, is brutal torment. So I led the young family into the kitchen.

I asked if the little ones were hungry. The younglings nodded, smiled briefly, and quickly dove back into the armpit of the Care Bear T-shirt. I gave them each a sandwich and some potato chips. Once they were settled, I walked outside toward the tool shed to see if I could locate a gas can. I searched the grounds for fuel canisters but could not find a single one.

During my quest, my New Orleans encounter with Eli materialized in my thoughts. I suddenly became overjoyed. I had been given yet another opportunity for atonement and a momentary escape from the facade of playing church. I rummaged through my wallet and saw that I had fifty dollars. I decided that this money was a sign from God that my aid was needed. My mind was made up. The canister and gasoline would be on me. In fact, I would serve as a chauffeur as well.

I went back inside with vibrance in my stride. I retrieved some toys and candy for the little ones from our children's area. Then I came back to the kitchen and presented the puzzles, chocolates, and Play-Doh on the table. Once the children were entertained, I excitedly informed the young couple of my decision. Jason was extremely grateful and offered to accompany me on the trip.

The drive was short, but my passenger had plenty to say about feeling blessed to be in the car instead of hiking for hours. Jason concluded that God had answered prayers in the middle of their difficult circumstance. Jason was quite the talker, and it turns out that this couple's recent sequence of events was complicated well before their decrepit GMC had run out of fuel.

Regrettably, this family recently was evicted from their home in South Carolina. They were forced to leave a double-wide trailer that harbored their family for three years. Recently their landlord died of a stroke. The landlord's children had inherited the property, and the new landlords had little desire to manage a decaying rental. They opted to sell both the land and the trailer, which meant that Jason and Krystal woke up the following week to a thirty-day eviction notice. Jason had to accept that the family had nowhere they could afford to go except to move in with Krystal's parents in northeastern Florida.

Strangely, as I was listening to this lamentable happenstance, my own frustration with my career had all but disappeared. It was odd, and quite inappropriate, to be affected this way in the midst of hearing someone else's turmoil, but I had stumbled upon meaning again. It was then that I realized that this pleasant sensation had twice emerged by making a difference for someone else in recent months.

"*This is what the Church should look like. Not a concert,*" I concluded.

Though I could no longer sense God's presence in an auditorium, I could perceive something heavenly in these opportunities for benevolence that were beginning to manifest in my life. Perhaps they were trying to tell me something?

We arrived at the Circle K gas station, quickly filled up two cans of gas, and made our way back to the church. Both of us had expressed a shared belief that God had ordained that moment, but our collective sense of appreciation for divine appointment would be short-lived.

As we pulled into the church parking lot we spotted Jason's family. They were sitting on the tailgate of their battered red pickup. They were unsheltered in the Deep South heat, and swatting at mosquitoes on their bare skin. Standing by their truck was my senior pastor who appeared to be less than pleased with the whole scenario and wore an expression that broadcasted a noticeable scowl.

Despite the evidence of my boss's frustration, I believed that my pastor would understand my actions if I explained myself. After all, I had done this for Jesus, and how could that be wrong? After all, the Gospel of Matthew says,

> for I was hungry and you gave me food, I was thirsty and you gave me something to drink, I was a stranger and you welcomed me, I was naked and you gave me clothing, I was sick and you took care of me, I was in prison and you visited me.' Then the righteous will answer him, 'Lord, when was it that we saw you hungry and gave you food, or thirsty and gave you something to drink? And when was it that we saw you a stranger and welcomed you, or naked and gave you clothing? And when was it that we saw you sick or in prison and visited you?' And the king will answer them, 'Truly I tell you, just as you did it to one of the least of these who are members of my family, you did it to me.'

So I came clean as I exited my vehicle and nervously began to disclose my reasoning for my actions.

"Sorry I left them unattended, Pastor. I didn't want to disturb you in your meeting. So I asked myself, 'What would Jesus do?' and I knew in that moment that Jesus would help this family in their time of need. It was an opportunity for evangelism. So I decided to feed them, and go get their gas," I explained.

Despite my devout explanation, my employer's grimace had not altered.

Sensing the tension between us, the couple apologized for any inconvenience, and reiterated that it was their belief that my aid was God's providence, and that God's hand had led them both to our church.

The pastor took a deep breath and retrieved a fat wallet full of cash from the confines of designer jeans. My message had gotten through!

The pastor fingered through the thick stack of bills that was stretching the seams of the brown leather wallet and pulled out approximately ten dollars. This minuscule offering was then presented to the family like it was a trophy to be cherished.

"I am happy to give this money to you, but I need you both to promise me that you won't use it for drugs," demanded my employer.

The sentence rang through my ears like a gunshot, and it had not just offended me. Jason and Krystal were visibly embarrassed, but they were desperate for financial help so they submitted to the so-called "pastor's" command. What little dignity Jason and Krystal had in their distress was stripped from them. By a minister of all people.

The entire grounds I had once believed to be sacred, had completely turned to shit before my eyes with no chance of redemption.

What scam had I devoted my life to? How could I ever have willingly nourished this parasitic organization with my talents? How was I ever convinced that this church's version of the Gospel of Jesus was "good news" for anyone other than themselves?

I could not fathom how I ever had previously viewed this leader, these grounds, this temple, and their teachings as anything other than a gigantic lie.

A massive amount of misinformation surrounds the concept of "The Gospel of Jesus."

The word "gospel" comes from the Koine Greek word *euangelion* and it literally means "good news." Most of my Christian life I was taught that the "good news" of Jesus was that Christ died for our sins so we can experience an eternal afterlife in "Heaven." For humans to be offered Christ's gift of immortality, we must confess that Jesus is our "lord and savior." Once we admit that Jesus is divine and was sacrificed to atone for our sins, then our souls are eternally secure in the next life.

Though this version of the "good news" of Jesus is certainly present in the Gospel of John, it is not present in the Gospels of Matthew, Mark, or Luke.

John's understanding of the gospel is a massive distortion of the good news that the historical Jesus preached. John's intentional alterations should not shock anyone, since John's Gospel was written almost a century after Christ died. Since Mark is the oldest of the four Gospels I often encourage my congregation to use Mark as the lens through which we interpret the other three Gospels.

I think that the best synopsis of the good news of Jesus in context can be extracted from the events surrounding the Passover Feast. Let's sequentially unpack these events in Mark starting with the triumphant entry:

> When they were approaching Jerusalem, at Bethphage and Bethany, near the Mount of Olives, he sent two of his disciples and said to them, "Go into the village ahead of you, and immediately as you enter it, you will find tied there a colt that has never been

ridden; untie it and bring it. If anyone says to you, 'Why are you doing this?' just say this, 'The Lord needs it and will send it back here immediately.'" They went away and found a colt tied near a door, outside in the street. As they were untying it, some of the bystanders said to them, "What are you doing, untying the colt?" They told them what Jesus had said; and they allowed them to take it. Then they brought the colt to Jesus and threw their cloaks on it; and he sat on it. Many people spread their cloaks on the road, and others spread leafy branches that they had cut in the fields. Then those who went ahead and those who followed were shouting,

"Hosanna! Blessed is the one who comes in the name of the Lord! Blessed is the coming kingdom of our ancestor David! Hosanna in the highest heaven!"

This story in Mark requires a slight bit of relearning for many evangelicals. Most Christians believe that Jesus rode a donkey into Jerusalem for the triumphant entry and not a colt. So where does this misconception about Jesus riding a donkey come from?

In the Gospel of Matthew, Jesus is said to have ridden a donkey and a colt at the same time in the author of Matthew's telling of this story.

That is absurd, if you think about it.

I grew up in the country and helped my dad train horses for years. You literally cannot sit on two saddles with one ass.

However, in the Gospels of Luke and Mark, there is no donkey in their telling of this story. Mark and Luke both say that Jesus rode a colt. So which was it?

I personally do not believe that there was a donkey involved in the actual events surrounding the triumphant entry, but I do believe that the Gospel of Matthew felt that Jesus riding a donkey was an important detail. Matthew had an intended audience that was Jewish, and there was a prophecy in the Old Testament found in the book of Zechariah that said,

Rejoice greatly, O daughter Zion!
Shout aloud, O daughter Jerusalem!
Lo, your king comes to you;
triumphant and victorious is he,
humble and riding on a donkey,
on a colt, the foal of a donkey.

Matthew wanted to convince a Jewish demographic that Jesus was the Messiah that was foretold, and that meant that all of the Old Testament prophecies about the coming Messiah needed to be fulfilled to get buy-in from Matthew's intended audience. Similar inconsistencies happen often in the Scriptures. Intentional alterations to Mark's narrative of Jesus occur many times throughout the Gospels of Matthew, Luke, and especially John, and these changes are always for a reason. We will discuss many scriptural inconsistencies throughout this book.

So, what is significant about Mark's telling of the triumphant entry having a young horse instead of a donkey?

First of all, the colt that the disciples "retrieved" was actually stolen, and it belonged to the governor of Rome.

How do we know the colt was smuggled to Jesus?

A few days before Passover, Rome would parade their military through Jerusalem to display their military might as a warning to all who dared to rebel against the empire. Every year Jewish people from far and wide would come to Jerusalem for the Passover ritual, and every year around this time Jewish rebels would attempt to lead an insurrection during this sacred event. Insurrectionists hoped that their violent uprising would be a catalyst for the massive amount of Jewish visitors in Jerusalem to join their campaign to banish their captors from their holy city. The Roman military parade was meant to act as a deterrent to these troublemakers by showing Jewish citizens exactly what they would be up against if they decided to rebel.

The star of this parade was the governor of Rome, and according to tradition, the governor would be mounted on a colt that was pure white.

Who was the governor?

Pontius Pilate.

So Jesus instructed two disciples to metaphorically steal the mayor's limousine, and if the disciples got caught, Jesus instructed them to lie and say that "The Lord" (aka Roman governor Pontius Pilate) had requested the colt be delivered by the disciples. Jewish citizens were often asked to serve the whims of governing officials, so no one would have thought twice about these two disciples fetching the colt for the governor.

The disciples brought the colt to Jesus, who then rode the governor's stolen parade mount into the city just before the Roman military parade began as a means of nonviolent subversion. Jewish onlookers saw this brave act of protest, and they cast their coats on the ground before Christ and shouted *"Hosanna."*

Hosanna is a Koine Greek translation of the Hebrew word *hoshiya na*. It is a cry for rescue that literally means "please save us."

From what entity was this Jewish crowd begging to be rescued?

The Roman Empire.

These Jewish citizens were asking Christ to defeat their captors.

The crowd's cry for help was the people's way of recognizing Jesus as a prophesied rebel leader whom they believed would one day arrive to defeat their Roman enemy. This foretold hero was known as their "Messiah."

This means that the triumphant entry was not a parade. It was an act that challenged the authority of the Roman government.

After this triumphant entry, Jesus and the disciples left the city for one night and returned to Jerusalem the next day. On the way back into the city something interesting happened. The book of Mark says,

> On the following day, when they came from Bethany, Jesus was hungry. Seeing in the distance a fig tree in leaf, he went to see whether perhaps he would find anything on it. When he came to it, he found nothing but leaves, for it was not the season for figs. He said to it, "May no one ever eat fruit from you again." And his disciples heard it.

This passage on its own is a peculiar story. Jesus noticed that a fig tree was not in season, and cursed it. This curse hardly seems fair to the fig tree. After all, it was only functioning as nature intended. On the surface Jesus killing the fig tree for not having ripe fruit when the tree was out of season appears to be more of a childish tantrum than a profound metaphor. But like other biblical narratives, there is much more going on than meets the eye.

The institution of Judaism that Jesus adhered to had been co-opted by Roman ideology, procedure, and policy. Similar to how American Christianity has been corrupted by the influence of Right Wing extremism today, this infiltration of imperial values in the temple royally pissed Jesus off.

But what the hell did Roman influence in the temple have to do with a fig tree?

The fig tree was an institutional symbol of ancient Judaism and was depicted on many banners in the temple. Jesus wasn't cruelly cursing a tree. For all intents and purposes Jesus was burning their flag on the way to cleanse their temple of economic injustice.

After Jesus "burned the flag," Jesus went to the temple to stir shit up:

> *Then they came to Jerusalem. And he entered the temple and began to drive out those who were selling and those who were buying in the temple, and he overturned the tables of the money changers and the seats of those who sold doves; and he would not allow anyone to carry anything through the temple. He was teaching and saying, "Is it not written,*
>
> *'My house shall be called a house of prayer for all the nations'?*
>
> *But you have made it a den of robbers."*
>
> *And when the chief priests and the scribes heard it, they kept looking for a way to kill him; for they were afraid of him, because the whole crowd was spellbound by his teaching. And when evening came, Jesus and his disciples went out of the city.*

In the early years of my career, I was taught that this temple cleansing was due to God's opposition of anyone auctioning any item within a sanctuary. It wasn't until years later that I would ascertain the complex layers of this story that give it a far deeper meaning.

I always pictured this temple being a 200- to 300-seater facility, but my ignorance failed to grasp both the enormity of the temple, and just how much effort was exuded by Jesus to cleanse it. Some modern scholars estimate that the people visiting Jerusalem for the Passover Feast was well over 300,000 Jewish people.

300,000 people!

All needing 300,000 animals to sacrifice.

That is a shit-ton of animals, and I pity those who were responsible for maintaining the courtyard, because that was probably a shit-ton of shit.

But why did that shit matter?

Because the space required to house that many animals meant that the courtyard was gargantuan!

This sacred building was located on top of the Temple Mount, and had over thirty acres in the courtyard alone. This acreage was reserved for livestock that would be offered during worship as well as hundreds of money changing tables that were used to sell sacrificial animals to Jewish people that did not bring an animal to sacrifice.

People who lived in close proximity to Jerusalem would bring their own livestock to atone for their sins. However, folks who traveled great distances to the temple often had to purchase animals when they arrived in Jerusalem. It simply wasn't practical to go on a long journey with livestock through the desert. To accommodate this need, the temple in Jerusalem would conveniently have birds, lambs, cattle, and other animals in the courtyard for visitors to purchase.

This is where things get tempestuous.

Erected outside the temple gates stood statues of eagles as a reminder of Rome's political dominance over the religious institution of

Judaism. These stone depictions outside the temple complex of a tyrannical kingdom whose ancestors ascended to power through land theft and colonization was a source of justifiable animosity for many Jewish people. This frustration especially was understandable considering Rome had imposed enormous exchange rates on the sacrificial animals that were being purchased by Jewish attendees. Jewish people from neighboring regions were required to convert their coin from Roman currency to a Tyrian shekel with money changers in the temple courtyard. This is because Roman currency had depictions of Caesar on their coins, and images of "false gods" were forbidden in the temple. This did not offend Roman authorities because at the temple's tables Rome imposed their outrageous taxes.

Contrary to what I had been told at every evangelical church I had ever attended, the selling of animals at the temple for the Passover Feast was not the cause for the temple cleansing. The practice of selling sacrificial animals for a fair price had been going on for centuries at the temple. Unjust economic legislation was the source of Christ's public display of righteous anger.

The furious spectacle of Jesus was understandable because the Passover Feast is a ceremony that symbolizes God's punishment of the empire of Egypt, and it is a celebration of God saving those who were enslaved by it. In the Gospel of Mark, Jesus likely became distressed upon witnessing the imperial corruption of a ritual that is a reminder of God's eternal opposition to tyrant kingdoms and their rulers.

So upon seeing the unjust procedure of Roman exchange rates, Jesus started flipping tables. Tables full of Roman coin. These tables were not just a few banquet-size tables like I once believed. This involved hundreds of enormous tables. Jesus marched through the courtyard spilling the contents of their registers. One by one Jesus scattered Roman coins bearing the engraved portrait of Caesar all over the temple grounds. By the time Christ had finished this uncivilized protest, Roman currency littered the entire mountainside, and there was nothing that Roman guards could do to stop this disruption, because Roman soldiers were not legally allowed to enter the temple grounds during Passover.

The fun doesn't stop here.

Jesus drove thousands of animals out of the temple by releasing them from their captivity. Jesus freeing the sacrificial animals significantly impeded the ceremony. This was not just an emotional outburst that frightened onlookers. Jesus intentionally hit Rome in its wallet. This act of disobedience was meant to get the attention of corrupted government and religious officials. Many historians believe that this protest is partially what encouraged Pilate to crucify Jesus.

At this point, you might be thinking to yourself, "*Wow, this is very similar to the Occupy Wall Street protests.*"

And you would be right!

While the animals were being driven out by the hundreds, Jesus accused the temple of becoming a "den of robbers." This is a direct quote from the book of Jeremiah. What is intriguing about the following quotation from Jeremiah is that, in context, this ancient passage was also a rebuke of religious leaders and governing officials.

Jeremiah 7 says,

> *For if you truly amend your ways and your doings, if you truly act justly one with another, if you do not oppress the alien, the orphan, and the widow, or shed innocent blood in this place, and if you do not go after other gods to your own hurt, then I will dwell with you in this place, in the land that I gave of old to your ancestors*

forever and ever. Here you are, trusting in deceptive words to no avail. Will you steal, murder, commit adultery, swear falsely, make offerings to Baal, and go after other gods that you have not known, and then come and stand before me in this house, which is called by my name, and say, "We are safe!"—only to go on doing all these abominations? Has this house, which is called by my name, become a den of robbers in your sight? You know, I too am watching, says the Lord.

"Baal" was a Semitic god worshiped by a Canaanite cult. The name "Baal" means "lord." This God was cruel, oppressive, and demanded the sacrifice of innocents. By quoting the verse in Jeremiah above Jesus was essentially comparing the empire of Rome to the corrupt cult of Baal.

These passages prove that Jesus was trying to be a voice for those who suffered in the wake of colonizers. Throughout the Gospel, Christ consistently and relentlessly shamed leaders for inequity, and chastised those in power for inflicting hardship on others.

Unfortunately for evangelical Christians, this contradicts their assumptions about the Gospel of Jesus. They have been told that the Gospel is a list of beliefs concerning Christ's divinity that others must "accept in their hearts." If they refuse to do so, then they will suffer the flames of eternal hellfire. According to evangelicals, once humans intellectually ascend to a fundamental knowledge of Jesus as our eternal savior, then we can be welcomed into the "kingdom of Heaven." Evangelicals spend hundreds of millions of dollars constructing worship spaces that are designed to communicate this erroneous version of the Gospel of Jesus.

My question is this: How is a theology based in the eternal torment of nonbelievers cohesive with Jesus' teachings in the New Testament? Humanity is required to "turn the other cheek" and "pray for our enemies," but Jesus will cleanse the enemies of God with everlasting fire? This "Messiah" would be a bloodthirsty tyrant, not a savior.

Luckily, historians make it clear that the fundamentalist view of life after death was not the belief of the early church.

The earliest followers of Christ were Jewish, and they did not have an evangelical understanding of the afterlife. They believed that the righteous and the unrighteous ended up in the same location after they pass away. Meaning, "Heaven and Hell" were both in the same place. They believed that Heaven and Hell were not binary eternal destinations assigned in the next life, but rather a conscious decision we will make to accept or reject the ultimate culture of love that will reign supreme in their God's eternal kingdom. In their view of Heaven and Hell, the landscape of the next life is unchanging, but our individual morality and ideology will affect how we experience life after death.

This belief system can be better explained in Rabbi Haim's "*The Allegory of the Spoons*":

> *One day a child said to God, "God, I would like to know what Heaven and Hell are like."*
>
> *God showed two doors. Inside the first one, in the middle of the room, was a large round table with a large pot of stew. It smelled delicious and made the child's mouth water, but the people sitting around the table were thin and sickly. They appeared to be famished. They were holding spoons with very long handles and each found it possible to reach into the pot of stew and take a spoonful, but because the handle was longer than their arms, they could not get the spoons back into their mouths.*
>
> *The child shuddered at the sight of their misery and suffering. God said, "You have seen Hell."*

Behind the second door, the room appeared exactly the same. There was the large round table with the large pot of wonderful stew that made the child's mouth water. The people had the same long-handled spoons, but they were well nourished and plump, laughing and talking.

The child said, "I don't understand."

God smiled. "It is simple," God said. "Love only requires one skill. These people learned early on to share and feed one another. While the greedy only think of themselves ..."

Jesus takes this understanding of the afterlife a step further by challenging the disciples not to wait for a manifestation of eternal paradise after death. When Jesus spoke of "Heaven and Hell," it was referencing the potential for alternate realities around us. Christ was not concerned with saving people from damnation in the next life when so many were going through Hell in this life. This means that the Gospel of Jesus was reassurance that one day tyranny will end, and justice will reign on Earth in a kingdom called "Heaven."

That is inspiring but sadly, just like in the *Allegory of the Spoons*, what would be Heaven to some would be Hell to others. In our depraved world, the Gospel of Jesus isn't "good news" for everyone. Good news to the poor is bad news for the billionaire. Good news for the slave is bad news for the master. Good news for the downtrodden is bad news for the sexist, the racist, and the homophobe. Good news for the environment is bad news for industry. Good news for the victim is bad news for the victimizer. Good news to the people is bad news to the powerful, and good news for the philanthropist is bad news for the extremist.

The Gospel of Jesus, if preached correctly, is both a message of freedom for the downtrodden, and a declaration of moral warfare to social consciences that create both the captive and captor in our society.

I am not condoning violence. The battles we must wage are not against flesh and blood, but rather the struggle before all Christ followers is to engage in a campaign against culture, and legislation, that make fatal combat appear unavoidable to those who are oppressed. The Gospel of Jesus calls for a social revolution, and though it must not be violent, it must be radical.

The notion of Christ's ideological warfare is reiterated in the passages in Mark directly preceding the events of the temple cleansing:

> In the morning as they passed by, they saw the fig tree withered away to its roots. Then Peter remembered and said to him, "Rabbi, look! The fig tree that you cursed has withered."

So when the disciples leave the city following the temple cleansing, they notice the fig tree that Jesus had cursed on the way into Jerusalem had withered and died. The flag of religious institution, the fig tree, had officially been symbolically burned. Then Jesus tells them,

> "Have faith in God. Truly I tell you, if you say to this mountain, 'Be taken up and thrown into the sea,' and if you do not doubt in your heart, but believe that what you say will come to pass, it will be done for you. So I tell you, whatever you ask for in prayer, believe that you have received it, and it will be yours.

Think about their geographic location when Jesus made this statement. When Jesus refers to a faith that can "move a mountain," the mountain in question happened to be the Temple Mount which hosted the Passover ritual. The same temple that Jesus had just protested and disrupted moments before. Jesus was saying that this "temple" (aka corrupted institutional religion) could even be "thrown into the sea" if necessary.

What was significant about Jesus saying that the temple could be thrown into "the sea"?

According to ancient Jewish belief, large bodies of water happened to be where demons and other hellish creatures like "Leviathan" lived. Essentially, Jesus was saying that both religion and empire could go to Hell where they belong, and we the people possess the power to banish them both.

Jesus was a BAMF!

That night of the Passover Feast, Jesus met with the disciples, broke unleavened bread, and poured out some wine to share.

Have you ever wondered why Jesus chose wine and bread as the sacraments for communion?

Wine and bread were the two most affordable elements of the Passover ritual. The new sacraments that Jesus selected would be used in lieu of a sacrificial lamb.

Why would Christ not eat a Passover lamb during this sacred feast? Was the first communion meant to abolish judaic sacrificial practices? Was Jesus saying that the disciples would no longer need to slaughter a lamb to atone for their sins?

That is exactly what Jesus was saying, but not for the reasons you have heard.

Christ altered the elements for their Passover ritual as a visual tool to convince the disciples to boycott purchasing all sacrificial animals from the temple in the future.

Why?

Rome had been profiting from imperial exchange rates at the money changers' tables. So communion was not some mystical memorial meal that could cleanse the disciples' souls. Communion was a symbolic protest of the injustices that developed after the merger of church and state.

Consequently, communion also is the only liturgical component of our modern-day worship services that also was practiced by the early church. Unfortunately, many people have forgotten its politically subversive origins.

For me, these stories summarize the true Gospel of Jesus. An accurate description of the good news of Christ may not be what you have heard, but it is undeniable that the Gospel is badass in context.

Regrettably, the good news of Jesus is currently so misunderstood in America that the Church has forgotten its purpose in waging ideological warfare against oppressive principalities, immoral profiteering, and corrupt authorities to the point that we have endorsed governing officials with those exact values from our nation's pulpits.

Donald Trump was asked to sign Bibles as if Trump was the author. Evangelicals thought that this was an amazing gesture. If adherents of Christianity celebrate our tyrannical emperor signing our sacred texts that contain accounts of a rabbinic rebel that was crucified by corrupt empire, then Christendom has failed the American people.

In this knowledge, It is time for Christians to declare that the time for nefarious administration in this country is up. It is time for followers of Christ to reclaim our mandated identity as prophets of equality. We must once again become a people unafraid to speak inconvenient truth to the cruel, the debauched, and the ignorant that presently sit elevated in our halls of business, governance and worship.

⬅—◄ ►—➡

Jason, a once elated individual grateful to receive an act of charity, departed from our sanctuary grounds defeated and insulted. It would seem that their brief miracle had morphed into a curse. When their vehicle was out-of-sight and the sputtering of their partially functioning engine could no longer be heard, the "pastor" started to lecture me on the proper policy of allowing entrance to "outsiders."

I interrupted my scolding with my formal resignation.

I did not know the trajectory of my career, but I knew where the values that shaped that spiritual community came from, and it certainly wasn't from the good news of Jesus. If the treatment of this family in need was a reflection of this "church's" understanding of the Gospel of Jesus, then it could go back to Hell where it belonged.

IDOLS

"You can do this, you idiot," I murmured quietly to my troubled reflection in the bathroom mirror.

There wasn't one unsaturated thread on my shirt due to my anxious perspiration. I was the most nervous I had ever been in the entirety of my career. I had performed musically for large audiences for years. I also had actively contributed to discussions in my weekly small group. But for me to give a half-hour presentation in front of a hundred parishioners was an unfamiliar duress.

Years after my resignation, I no longer was seeking employment by megachurches. I had received job offers that were quite lucrative from larger churches in their youth and music departments, but I rejected these opportunities because those communities appeared to have similar hypocritical values to the parasitic church I had left. I wanted something fresh. I longed to offer my life to an organization that served the spiritual needs of the populace, but that also met the physical needs of those seeking public assistance. That is when I discovered what evangelicals call "missional churches." A missional church is a church on mission to serve their community.

After some major Google searching, I located a church in a neighboring county that was in need of a music minister. About a year after my employment, I was asked to do a presentation on "worship" during a Sunday service. This was logical being that I was the music director. So I began to research the origins of Christian liturgy, and in my pursuit of studying the original meaning of "worship" in the early church, I became fearful for my career. Not only did I discover that the early church was nothing like a concert, it was nothing like any church I had ever been a part of.

Turns out in preparing for this sermon I uncovered that there were no "worship pastors" in the early church. NONE! In fact, biblical "worship" didn't have a damn thing to do with music at all. Which, by the way, is not great news if you are employed as the worship leader!

The word "liturgy" comes from the Greek term *leitourgia*. It is formed by two root words: *laos* ("people") and *ergon* ("work"). The word literally means "work of the people." So a better translation of an ancient worship service would be "public service."

This knowledge led to many other questions. If early Christian liturgy was more about social work than a spiritual experience, where did these cathedrals, prayers, creeds, and hymns come from? I spent countless hours in research and consultation with my friends who were enrolled in seminary.

Once again, the culprit was Rome. When Rome nationalized Christianity, it kidnapped the theology of the growing populace of Jewish Christ followers and fashioned it into the existing framework of Roman worship.

Pagan temples became cathedrals, Roman gods depicted in those sanctums became saints, and elements of Roman mythology were injected into the Christian Scriptures in an attempt to receive public approval from both the pagan Roman populace and the Jewish followers of Christ. This merging of worship components was politically brilliant. This sanctioned assimilation was enacted in order to prevent a splintering society from fracturing entirely. Metaphorically Rome was losing power due to several complex factors after Christ's death while the early church continued to expand its influence. This ultimately required the empire to change its identity. So Rome nationalized Christianity, and those in power began to meddle with the early church liturgy. What exists today is a merger of Roman practices, imperial values, and severely altered tenants of the early church. All three of these attributes have been blended with varying fruits of pagan appropriation, and that is the origin of most Christian traditions. In short, empire colonized Christian liturgy.

Even the Trinity was adopted from pagan beliefs. Trinitarianism, the belief that God is three-in-one, cannot be found in the Bible. The early Christians were Jewish, and they were monotheistic. Therefore, they only believed in a singular god.

Trinitarianism originated from the assimilation of ancient imperial deities from many ancient empires into church theology. Ancient Roman scholars noticed that history's greatest civilizations—the Sumerians, Babylonians, Egyptians, and Greeks—had gods that were in a trinity.

This unbiblical theological construct especially was useful when attempting to appeal to conquered Celtic tribes. Celts often worshiped spirits that, according to their oral traditions, presented themselves in groups of three. After the nationalization of Christendom to make Christianity more palatable to conquered Celtic warrior tribes, the Church really pushed a theology of the Trinity to appease subjugated citizens.

This should not surprise anyone. Christendom basically did the same thing with our Christmas and Easter rituals.

During this time of study, I discovered that much of Christian "tradition" is just repackaged paganism.

I also stumbled upon another interesting fact. Current congregational titles present in almost every denomination are far from biblical. Which fascinated me until I remembered that I was about to go on stage in front of our pastor, my boss, and point out that the concept of modern clerical titles are not only unbiblical, they can be downright harmful.

The word "pastor" comes from the Koine Greek word *poimén.* Though we presently use this word as a noun, its original meaning also was a verb used to describe the duties of a shepherd. Meaning a biblical "pastor" is someone who attends to the welfare of a community. It was not used to distinguish a spiritual hierarchy between clergy and laity. But leave it to the Roman Empire to royally fuck shit up.

"Clergy" was a common phrase in Rome that comes from the latin word *clerici,* and it means "learned or appointed person." This definition appears to be relatively benign until we examine the Latin word "laity."

"Laity" was a term used to describe congregants. These were the unlearned masses. The word "laity" comes from the Latin phrase *idiota,* and it literally means "idiot." Needless to say, this is not a class structure that I believe the historical Jesus would have endorsed.

This was all fascinating until I remembered that I was presenting this information in front of my pastor, who also happened to be the same person who signed my check every week.

So there I was, a terrified *idiota* about to go on stage and tell the entire congregation that our symbols, creeds, and ministerial job descriptions all were technically unbiblical. I was preparing myself for my first, and in all probability, last sermon. Still, I was resolved in my conviction that this obscure knowledge should be distributed. I stood in front of the mirror staring at my anxious expression knowing that this presentation likely would terminate my employment with this church.

My incessant pursuits of revitalizing early Christian practices were starting to be a pain in my ass.

Traditional liturgical components do not appeal to the mass majority of young people in Western society.

There is a multitude of reasons as to why this lack of interest occurs, but the themes that are consistently presented to me by non-Christians is that worship spaces, creeds, rituals, and the language of church is either irrelevant or incredibly traumatic to many young people outside the Christian faith.

Many people have been scarred by the church. I guarantee that those reading this book have either been damaged by the Christian faith themselves, or at minimum know someone who was. Because of this, our ancient symbols, robed attire, candle-filled altars, and congregations fluent in their "church speak" are reminiscent of spiritual wounds. If by chance traditional aspects of worship do not remind non-Christians of a painful past, they almost certainly incite negative assumptions that are associated with evangelical belief.

I suggest that public discomfort likely was unavoidable if we consider the imperial entity that created these relics.

Empire and religion should never mix, nor should we pay homage to the fruits of their marriage, so why does the Church continue to honor the legacy of their merger today?

Even if these artifacts and customs are located in liberal houses of spirituality, they still make many former victims of Christian fundamentalism uncomfortable. I am aware that many of us enjoy these traditions and symbols, but nostalgia isn't a good enough reason for these relics to endure.

I would like to offer another story that I believe will perfectly capture my point.

My spouse and I met on a dating app in 2016. I entered the digital dating world cynical and jaded. Ali had little faith in the institution of marriage and, at the time, had no desire in seeking a lifelong commitment.

But one night while browsing the electronic pool of single adults within a ten-mile radius, I noticed this gorgeous brunette, and after days of chatting we knew quite a lot about one another. Choice foods, our favorite colors, travel experiences, our preferred taste in films, and our Hogwarts houses. But I refused to inform Ali about what I did for a living.

Why?

Because when people find out that I am a minister they will either,

A) Distance themselves because they paint me with the same brush as Joel Osteen, and assume that I am trying to convert, rob, and/or abuse them.

Or

B) Refrain from using foul language or watching R rated films in my presence in an attempt to make me comfortable, because they assume that all ministers are lame.

Neither one of these frequent occurrences appealed to me when I joined the online dating world.

The cryptic answers I gave about my professional life certainly concerned Ali. I think Ali sincerely believed that I may have either been a drug dealer, or an assassin. Ali texted curiosities about my job frequently, and I would simply respond by saying that I could not disclose that information at that point in time.

I was hoping that these messages would come across as "mysterious," but Ali assured me that it came across like a plotline from a *Breaking Bad* episode.

After a few days of chatting nonstop online, we decided to meet in person.

Unfortunately for us, the bar we initially met at was packed. Luckily, there was another restaurant a few blocks away with a similar menu, so I offered to escort Ali down for a bite.

I opened the passenger door of my Prius, which Ali didn't hesitate to mock, and walked around to the driver's side. I got into the driver's seat, fastened my seatbelt, adjusted my rearview mirror, and just before I pressed the ignition button, I glanced over to see how beautiful Ali looked one more time. As I rotated my head, I noticed that Ali's prior expression of excitement had now turned to horror. My date's wandering eyes had located the crucifix necklace that decorated my rearview mirror. Ali was no longer curious with my occupation. It was clear that Ali now was only deeply concerned about my religion.

"Oh no! You aren't religious, are you?" Ali asked, deeply troubled.

This was the first time I had ever heard a gagging sound assimilated into the recitation of the word "religious."

"Fuck no!" I said emphatically. "But I am a pastor," I laughed nervously.

I had hoped my humor would help ease the tension.

It didn't.

Ali wasn't amused. My partner had not realized how hilarious I was at this point in our relationship. After almost three years together, I still am waiting patiently for my spouse to arrive at this conclusion.

I began to unpack how much my belief system differed from what many people considered to be "Christian beliefs."

At first Ali wasn't entirely convinced that my faith was genuinely different than what Ali had experienced in the past. My now nervous date explained that there were many reasons they chose to remain firmly agnostic with zero desire to EVER convert.

Now I was curious, so I asked what those reasons were.

Ali had grown up attending a conservative Lutheran church in Michigan. Not only had worship bored Ali to tears, but Ali's entire family had traumatic experiences in church when Ali was growing up. They were each told on multiple occasions that they were going to Hell for multiple reasons. Circumstances like not attending church on a regular basis, or not sharing their musical talents with the congregation on Sunday mornings had secured Ali, and the entire family, a one-way ticket to an eternal fiery furnace.

My seemingly harmless rearview mirror relic made of wood and faux leather had shaken the dynamic of our entire evening. The cross had transported Ali back to an inner place of fear, and there was nothing I could have done with the cross that would have altered Ali's negative perception about my belief system.

Can you imagine what it would have been like for Ali to physically walk into a sanctuary at this stage of our relationship? It took months before Ali would feel comfortable enough to attend a worship service with me and, to this very day, Ali is still slightly uncomfortable with religious symbolism.

There is a tremendous amount of agony associated with Christian symbolism, church speak, traditions, and aesthetics, and it is time for us to not only acknowledge this, but we must also do something to remedy it. No matter the intent of fellow believers and our ministers, many people never will be able to discover value in most Christian traditions and our traditional symbolism.

Let's use the Jesus fish (aka *ichthys*) as another example. The *ichthys* was originally a far more exciting symbol than just a tacky magnet for cars. We easily can spot these metallic emblems in traffic on any given day. I guarantee that most of the populace using this fish to decorate their vehicles as a public statement of faith have no idea about its badass origin story. I also can safely wager from my own anecdotes that many displaying the Jesus fish on the exterior of their automobiles do not act very Christ-like behind the wheel.

I once was flipped off by a person who had not one, but a school of five Jesus fish scattered about their tailgate. This person was so skilled in the usage of this crude gesture that they accomplished a twin one-gun salute with both hands off the wheel while maintaining their speed and trajectory.

Quite frankly, I was far more impressed with this ability than offended by it.

But I digress.

The usage of the *ichthys* predates the cross in church history. It was a symbol for the underground aspect of the early church before Christianity was nationalized. The church began in the shadows, and the *ichthys* fish was utilized as a secret handshake of sorts while Christians were being persecuted by Romans.

A scenario for its usage may have gone something like this:

If you were a Jewish follower of Christ in hiding, and you were in desperate need of supplies or possibly a safe house, then in all likelihood you would have to seek out allies for assistance. The only complication besides your circumstance was that you couldn't broadcast this need audibly in public. Early Christians needed to be absolutely sure that they were safe before they confessed their faith to a stranger.

So let's say that you elected to visit a bustling market to blend in with the crowd and look for assistance. You decide to strike up a conversation with a local merchant. At some point in the dialogue, you run your finger through the dust on the merchant's table like so:

If they were not privy to the inner workings of the early church, then this merchant may just assume that you were bored with the conversation, uninterested in their wares, or perhaps a bit strange. However, if the merchant was "in the know" as a compassionate ally, or better yet, if they were also part of this underground society, then the merchant would complete the symbol by drawing the rest of the fish in the dust like so:

That is some seriously subversive badassery going on in this fish. All of this brilliant ancient underground resistance packed into a logo that a toddler could reproduce.

Despite how fascinating the history of this symbol is, it doesn't alter the fact that today this once underground symbol of disruption has been commandeered by empire and institution to spread their intolerant manifestos. Many folks outside the Church have no desire to be associated with any space that displays Christian insignias regardless of their origins.

Society's unwillingness to reclaim a logo that has been used to harm others is nothing new. Before Nazis claimed the swastika in the 1930s, it was a symbol of good luck in western cultures. Prior to that, the swastika was a positive spiritual design throughout India and Asia. In some cultures it still is.

Even though this emblem experienced a benign history prior to the rise of fascism in Nazi Germany, it NEVER would be considered appropriate for anyone to reclaim the swastika as a wholesome symbol today. Too much devastation has been enacted under this insignia. It may have had a positive message prior to Nazis hijacking it, but it will continue to be a painful reminder to many people well into the future.

So it is with robes, stained glass, steeples, crosses, pews, and hymnals. Despite their original message, notwithstanding their intent, and regardless of our own positive ambitions, these traditions, artifacts, and symbols have been banners historically used to unite fundamentalists in their march of oppression. If we want to present a message that vastly differentiates us from the corrupt and bigoted rationalities of Christendom's past, then we cannot use benchmarks and banners from church history. These historical footnotes cannot be reclaimed no matter how pure our intentions may be.

Many may disagree with me, but it is my opinion that there is nothing that we can do to reclaim these artifacts, methods, and symbols of antiquity successfully. There is no remedy that can undo the trauma experienced or understood by the masses who have justifiably fled the Christian faith.

There is a section of sacred text found in Isaiah:

> *bringing offerings is futile;*
> *incense is an abomination to me.*
> *New moon and sabbath and calling of convocation—*
> *I cannot endure solemn assemblies with iniquity.*
> *Your new moons and your appointed festivals*
> *my soul hates; they have become a burden to me,*
> *I am weary of bearing them.*
> *When you stretch out your hands,*
> *I will hide my eyes from you;*
> *even though you make many prayers,*
> *I will not listen; your hands are full of blood.*
> *Wash yourselves; make yourselves clean;*
> *remove the evil of your doings*
> *from before my eyes;*
> *cease to do evil, learn to do good;*
> *seek justice, rescue the oppressed,*
> *defend the orphan, plead for the widow.*

Perhaps the Divine has grown tired of our liturgical traditions, and would much rather that we simply use our efforts to pursue justice, peace, and charity while cultivating new practices for meditation, inspiration, and reflection that are not triggering to the general public.

If the God of the Bible is constructed of love in its entirety as depicted in the ancient texts, it stands to reason that loving our neighbor and seeking a future that distributes abundance equally among all of God's children is the most worshipful thing that those who believe in this God can achieve. Those of us in the Christian faith can construct new liturgical methods of conducting worship that completely surrender the painful baggage of Christianity's past.

Besides, if we think about it logically, all traditions were new at one point in time.

Looking back, I must admit that the execution of my sermon was hideous. When it came to public speaking, I didn't know what the hell I was doing. Luckily, the interesting content in my presentation was enough to encourage several congregants to ask questions about my research. They even asked me to suggest materials for further reading about authentic worship in the early church. I was thrilled about these inquiries. Perhaps this dialogue about modern Christian community going astray from its historical roots, and the knowledge that many Christian traditions and symbols are triggering, would spark a conversation in how our community could be a leading voice in a new reformation of the Church.

The following Tuesday my pastor informed me that I was immediately being let go. My teaching was considered to be heretical, and the pastor requested that I reconsider my calling as a minister.

How could I be a heretic for educating Christians about a time when our faith was more authentic?

Years later I happened upon a song by Trevor Morgan that reminds me how far the Church has strayed from the path of biblical worship.

> *Jesus rides the subway*
> *With the "junkies and the freaks"*
> *Jesus rides the subway*
> *With the "hustlers and the creeps"*
> *rubs shoulders with the thieves*
> *And looks a lot like everyone we see*
> *Yeah, Jesus rides the subway*
> *While the pretty people sleep*
> *Jesus went to church on Sunday*
> *Sat in the back and sang the hymns*
> *Jesus went to church on Sunday*
> *But they didn't recognize Him*

SAMARITANS

The tension in the room was thick as I remained unmoved by the insults that were hurled at me by an unknown red-faced baby boomer who decided to crash our young adult Bible study.

I was a guest speaker, and due to an unexpected explosive debate I had gone over my allotted time by about thirty minutes. My mismanagement was unintentional, but it could not be helped because I constantly had to address every point made by a handful of infuriated zealots.

My topic of discussion was "Loving Your Muslim Neighbor." Apparently, teaching a theology of tolerance was something that this conservative baby boomer wasn't willing to tolerate.

"You mean to tell me that if a Muslim were to show up here tonight that we should all just welcome them in with open arms and offer to share our coffee and snacks with them?" the red-faced Pharisee snarled.

"According to the New Testament, Jesus would have done so, and I would argue that Christ would instruct us to do so much more than just feed them," I countered firmly.

I was flawless in the execution of my rebuttal. The timing, my vocal inflection, the whole package of a mic drop was there. I thought my statement was a slam dunk, but my arrogant assumptions about my ability to augment opposing mindsets would soon be proven to be inaccurate. After my comeback, I scanned the room only to witness a few people in agreement with my perspective. Most attendees were shaking their heads negatively and whispering harsh words of criticism. One description I overheard about my sermon was,

"This is some hippie-dippie New Age horse shit."

Enthused by the conservatism in the room, the heckler stood up, pointed to me, and said, "Welcoming Muslims in our churches is not biblical, and if that is what you are teaching about the Bible then, Christopher, you truly are a heretic."

That label no longer bothered me. After years of this insult being hurled at my character, I was getting strangely comfortable with this title. Though the intention behind conservative name-calling can be painful, labels of blasphemy distributed by organizations of bigotry are something to embrace.

After I was let go from my position as worship leader as described in the last chapter, I began to dive deeper into scriptural meaning.

I became an avid reader of all things theology. The more I learned, the more progressive I became and the more offensive my views were to the majority of the Christians that I knew. I now call this unfortunate but inevitable chain reaction "the devout paradox."

My presentation was an attempt to dip my audience's toe into a moderate alternative to their twisted version of a Republican Jesus. I hadn't explained why I no longer believed Genesis was literal. I hadn't illustrated how I concluded that LGBTQ folks could identify as Christians regardless of their sexuality. I had not distinguished myself as a monotheist and explained that I no longer identified as a Trinitarian. I simply had instructed them to love strangers, orphans, and widows. These principles are the most basic of the core tenants of Christ's teachings, and they looked at me as if I had horns on my head, a pitchfork in my hands, and a spiked tale swinging from my ass crack.

Regrettably there are times you cannot win the opposition over, and it is difficult to leave those moments without a notion of defeat. That is exactly what happened to me after this taxing exchange. So after the Bible study concluded, I went to a nearby restaurant with a bar to de-stress.

I sat on a sticky stool fuming over my recent debate. I Googled random articles on my Razr flip phone in an attempt to collect my thoughts. I gestured to the end of the bar for a refill and the bartender poured another Newcastle Brown Ale into my dirty pint glass.

(Forgive me. The only aspects of my persona that have evolved more than my theological stances over the years is my taste in beer. In my defense, I would have had to travel a great distance to get my hands on quality craft brew, so I had to make do.)

I attempted to absorb the digital content displayed on my device, but my efforts to de-stress were in vain. I quickly chugged my ale and ordered a third round. That is when I heard these infuriating words emanating from behind my barstool:

"You want to know how I am positive that your message tonight was garbage?" an annoyingly familiar voice interrogated.

I took a breath, sighed, turned 180 degrees, exhaled, and with a sarcastic chuckle I said, "Enlighten me."

With a forced smile on my face, I acknowledged the obnoxious presence of two of my esteemed opponents from earlier that night were now having dinner at the booth behind me. What a lucky night this turned out to be.

"Your message was garbage because you are the kind of Christian that claims to follow the Bible, but then you retreat to a place like this to drink beer all night long. Maybe if you actually read your Bible you wouldn't be spreading lies and sitting at the bar drinking that mess," my critic proselytized with palpable arrogance.

"Really?" I asked, mockingly.

Years of people implying that I was a wolf in sheep's clothing had gone unchallenged long enough. I had my fill of playing nice, and it was time for closure.

I chugged the rest of my Newcastle for extra measure and placed the glass loudly on the bar. I covered my mouth with a closed fist, blew out a prehistoric belch, and smiled from ear to ear.

"So a couple things ...," I said as I slowly rose to my feet.

⊷—— ⊷

A few months prior to this irritating encounter, I was studying the Gospels and by chance happened upon a dissertation concerning the cultural tension of Samaritanism and Judaism during the time of Christ. The thesis compared the complex relationship between these two sects of Semitic religions to modern-day tensions between Christianity and Islam. Reading this educational material caused me to have an honest moment of self-examination. Due to massive amounts of misinformation, I unintentionally had been spreading Islamophobia for years.

The pulpit of every church I had ever worked for had been used to whip Christians into a frenzy about Islam. This intolerant ideology was/is a national epidemic. The church's fear-based propaganda worked so effectively that a majority of American Christians endorsed the criminal campaign of George W. Bush in the Middle East. I regret that I, like many other Christians, lapped this grotesque teaching up like a whipped dog.

This vicious ideology is still apparent at evangelical 9/11 memorials.

American Christians still convene on the Sabbath and honor the 2,977 lives taken from America on September 11th. Though I do not mean to diminish that loss at all, it is perplexing that what you do not hear from evangelical pulpits is anyone discussing the approximate 244,000 civilians killed in the Middle East as a result of the American military. Virtually no one in evangelical communities discusses the 10.1 million refugees that are a result of America's "War on Terror."

In the United States we call Islam terrorism, but in the Middle East Americans are the terrorists.

I still remember our 9/11 worship service back in my "Six Flags Over Jesus" days. It was a Trump supporter's wet dream come true, complete with American flag bulletins and red, white, and blue stage lighting. We used F-16 fighter jets depicted in video clips to encourage our congregation to pray for our troops. We designed 3-D digital assault rifles in the shape of a cross for power-point backgrounds in order to remind our parishioners of their Second Amendment rights. We played videos that compared Jesus dying for our sins, to modern-day American soldiers dying on the field of battle. We had actors who played ghosts of 9/11 victims and emergency responders. These performers notified our congregation that all American heroes died in vain if we don't fight the nation of Islam as "one Christian nation under God."

Sadly, this logic is still common in many churches today.

If evangelical fundamentalists erroneously believe that the United States was founded as a Christian nation, then someone should remind them that the Bible says to love our enemies, not bomb the hell out of their entire village! True Christianity is supposed to provide help for orphans and widows, not create them!

This is why the passage in Luke 10 concerning the Good Samaritan is important.

Just then a lawyer stood up to test Jesus. "Teacher," he said, "what must I do to inherit eternal life?" He said to him, "What is written in the law? What do you read there?" He answered, "You shall love the Lord your God with all your heart, and with all your soul, and with all your strength, and with all your mind; and your neighbor as yourself." And he said to him, "You have given the right answer; do this, and you will live."

But wanting to justify himself, he asked Jesus, "And who is my neighbor?" Jesus replied, "A man was going down from Jerusalem to Jericho, and fell into the hands of robbers, who stripped him, beat him, and went away, leaving him half dead. Now by chance a priest was going down that road; and when he saw him, he passed by on the other side. So likewise a Levite, when he came to the place and saw him, passed by on the other side. But a Samaritan while traveling came near him; and when he saw him, he was moved with pity. He went to him and bandaged his wounds, having poured oil and wine on them. Then he put him on his own animal, brought him to an inn, and took care of him. The next day he took out two denarii, gave them to the innkeeper, and said, "Take care of him; and when I come back, I will repay you whatever more you spend." Which of these three, do you think, was a neighbor to the man who fell into the hands of the robbers?" He said, "The one who showed him mercy." Jesus said to him, "Go and do likewise."

In the Talmud, the Samaritans are called "Cutheans." The term is derived from the city Kutha, which is geographically located in modern-day Iraq. Samaritanism is similar to Judaism, and it shares much of the same sacred texts. The most notable differences between them are that Samaritans believe that Mount Gerizim is God's chosen city, not Jerusalem. Samaritans also maintain a different variation of the Ten Commandments. If you were to compare the two faiths side by side overall, they would be extremely similar to one another. Kind of like the three major Abrahamic religions of today (Christianity, Judaism, and Islam) are incredibly similar to one another. This tension between faiths is why the parable of the Samaritan is so interesting.

There was a lot of hatred exchanged between the differing Abrahamic faith communities during the time of Christ. Some beliefs were more contemptuous to the Jewish people than others. Samaritanism was a top contender for the most loathed "heretics" of this age. In that same vein, Islam is tragically the most reviled of the three Abrahamic faiths in the world of evangelicalism today. It is the reason why so many Christians are anti-Palestine. Even with irrefutable evidence that the Palestinian people are being oppressed by Israeli legislation and occupation, many Christians support Israel. In fact, the largest American lobby for pro-Israeli policy, AIPAC, is largely funded by Christian Zionists.

Christian Zionism is the belief that the state of Israel's full control of Palestine is in accordance with biblical prophecy. Some even believe Israel having control of the Holy Land is a prerequisite for the second coming of Jesus. Many Christian Zionists believe that America will be cursed if we do not stand with Israel regardless of whether or not their political actions are ethical. Christian Zionists will stand with Israel's actions no matter how morally wrong Israeli policy may be to Muslim peoples.

This sad state of affairs was my exact reasoning for discussing this passage.

I attempted to use the Good Samaritan to explain to my peers that if Jesus were to appear before us and retell this parable using familiar religious institutions and imagery, I am fairly confident that the character portrayed as the Good Samaritan would be a Muslim. The characters neglecting the bloodied victim abandoned in the ditch would likely be an evangelical pastor and a Catholic priest.

I believe that Jesus was trying to make a point with this story. The moral here is that it is not what you believe that initiates your sanctification, but rather how you act on those beliefs. It is not for us to judge another's merit or virtue based on our faith identity. We must judge others based on whether their behavior is beneficial or harmful.

With that said, Christian bigotry against Islam is one of the most toxic attributes of evangelicalism.

Contrary to what many will say, this statement is NOT rooted in any form of anti-semitism. I acknowledge that the Christian faith has been one of the worst offenders of crimes against the Jewish people.

I admit that.

I am ashamed of that.

I pledge my life to make damn sure that the Church's committing of crimes against Jewish people never happens again on my watch.

However, we have to get to a place where we can distinguish between the disgusting cultural disease of anti-semitism and necessary criticism of Israel's current destructive policies against the people of Palestine. We can be critical of legislation without being intolerant of a differing religion.

American and Israeli governments do not get a free pass for harmful behavior. Being complicit in the face of tyrannical policies emerging from any nation is not part of the Christian praxis. In fact, shame on any faith leader who uses the Scriptures to manipulate adherents to passively accept the brutality of others. Being a voice for the voiceless is part of the Christian heritage, and standing between the afflicted and those that would do them harm is the legacy that Jesus intended to leave behind.

I conclude that we must cherish all that dwells on this planet regardless of their faith alignment. We must let compassion, peace, justice, and charity be our unifier. We can no longer allow our differing interpretations on matters that are spiritual divide us.

When injustice comes for any people, then followers of Christ must be the first to seek reparations. The Church must learn to love all of our neighbors as ourselves with our words and with our immediate intervention. Like it or not, every person, every nation, every tribe, and every faith community is our neighbor on this giant space rock we call Earth. It is time the Church acts like it and for humanity to takes action whenever it becomes necessary.

This means that the intolerance of anyone can no longer be tolerated in Christianity. Period.

<hr>

My mind was devoid of hesitation or fear. There was only hard truth seizing control of my lips, and these hypocrites needed to hear it.

"Bar and Grill is literally in the name of this establishment. If you have an issue with people drinking, maybe learn to read the goddamn sign outside the door, or at least don't sit next to the taps. But I dunno, I am not a doctor," I said sarcastically.

"But I suppose that requesting you two to read anything is expecting a little much. I couldn't even get you two to read scriptures that instruct you to love other people earlier without the two of you shitting a chicken, " I said, not allowing them to interject.

"Also, newsflash y'all. Jesus drank wine often. The first miracle in the Gospels was Christ making wine during a wedding where people were already shit-faced. Hell, I ain't even tipsy."

"And. Oh. My. God," I said looking down at their meals. "Is that what I think it is?"

"I find it hilarious that you are both being critical of anyone that drinks alcohol in moderation even though it is permissible in the Bible. Yet somehow in your righteous indignation you both ignored the Levitical laws that literally prohibit eating the shrimp and sausage in your Low Country boil," I said giggling as I pointed to their piping hot food.

"But that's the old cove...," they tried to counter before I interrupted them again.

"Bullshit. You're not Christians. You're modern-day Pharisees, and aside from that you're both just assholes, and you are both shining beacons of the shit pile that Christianity has become. So if you don't mind, I come in here occasionally to escape douche canoes that talk down to me.

"Might I suggest that if you wanna act like turds, you both take a walk outside and go lie in the grass. Otherwise, I hope you both can enjoy your plate full of Old Testament blasphemy and leave me the hell alone." I sat back down at the bar and signaled for another beer.

Where there was no support for me earlier that night at the young adult Bible study, I found that I had acquired a room full of admirers at this establishment. I heard several people slur "amen preacher" from the bar. Another table even clapped their hands.

One patron chimed in on my come-to-Jesus meeting by saying, "You two are the reason I am here on Sundays, and not in a pew. Everyone at this bar can smell your shit and it stinks."

"Yeah, we do not need your shit here. Y'all do us all a favor and leave in case the health inspector comes," the bartender demanded.

"I agree. You both should leave," I said firmly.

"You really put the Christ in Christopher. Seriously? What would Jesus do?" my opponent objected.

"Oh, you mean you don't enjoy feeling unwelcome because of your religious views? Imagine how a Muslim would have felt at your Bible study tonight," I said pointedly. "And to answer your WWJD question, Jesus would call you both a brood of vipers. However, you do have a point. Christ would still direct me to love you both even if you needed to be called out. So before you two snakes kick rocks, grab a to-go bag, and I will pay your bill. Oh, and God bless." I pointed to the bartender to put their food on my tab.

They knocked their plates on the floor and left in a huff. I experienced a weight off of my shoulders for the first time in months.

I had made a good impression on the people at the bar. I even made some new friends that night. Most of them were spiritual refugees drinking away their pain. I realized in this moment that I had been appealing to the wrong audience for quite some time.

In reflection later that night, I marked this occurrence as the first instance I had ever firmly stood my ground against evangelicals in their destructive ignorance. Though this was a monumental achievement, I promised myself for the sake of those at the bar and for my own self-care, that it would not be the last time I put my foot down to Christians if necessary.

This was just the beginning.

SODOMITES

I watched the sunrise as it slowly crept over the Low Country marsh grass. Egrets and herons glided in and out of the framework of this breathtaking landscape. A few feet away, a harbor porpoise emerged to inhale fresh morning air as it continued to patrol the perimeter of the dock searching for breakfast. Once again, the tidal creek before me abundantly provided the spiritual and physical needs of all creatures within its embrace.

I sat marveling at creation, with my phone in hand, dreading the call I soon would have to make.

It had been six years since my encounter with the Islamophobic baby boomers at the bar. This led me to examine many new opportunities in the realm of church employment and in my journey to discover my ministerial calling I finally had unearthed my purpose.

Church planting.

"Church planting" is a term that describes the art of starting new churches.

I was enthralled with the process and much happier in these innovative spaces. I adored the spirit of creativity that came with cultivating something fresh. I loved how these cutting-edge gatherings genuinely cared about reaching target demographics that were largely ignored by megachurches and traditional worship halls.

However, after years of leadership in the music department of multiple church plants, it became clear that church planting was not devoid of toxicity.

For example, some of these plants would be "welcoming to all people," but still were non-affirming to LGBTQ relationships. Instead of being openly hateful to diverse sexual/gender identities, these churches would politely condemn them as "sinners to be loved" from their small group curriculum instead of their pulpits. Oftentimes these open but non-affirming LGBTQ spaces are even more detrimental to people, because it gives the illusion of acceptance.

Other "church plants" I visited created endeavors to offer public assistance for single mothers, but wouldn't ordain women in their congregation.

Some of these new churches taught nonviolence socially, but were pro-war in their hermeneutics and homiletics.

Other models fed the poor during the week while ignorantly preaching that they believed that the early church created capitalism.

During this time in exploring "better" conservative church alternatives, I learned that achieving any improvement in regard to noxious fundamentalism was not a lofty standard.

My time in assisting evangelical church plants wasn't completely terrible, though. Even though the struggles within these communities were often incredibly irritating during this chapter of my life, some annoying occurrences were quite amusing.

One instance transpired during a pastoral meeting that still makes me laugh to this day.

A bunch of local church planters had gathered to discuss our congregational plans for the upcoming year. This meeting was intended to be a ministerial "think tank" of sorts, but I think logic must have missed the Evite, because it was rarely ever present.

For a group of folks that projected themselves as dynamic and engaging, they still submitted themselves to dated regulations for conducting their meetings. Robert's Rules of Order was second only to the King James in these circles. Because of this, I rarely was alert during these painfully boring sessions.

I look forward to the day when the mental torment of these meetings will be completely wiped from my memory, but there is one particular meeting that I can never forget. On this specific occasion, the pastor under whom I was serving gave a presentation that challenged all spiritual leaders present to reach beyond their congregation and serve their community at-large. This call to action was in response to a local survey conducted by HUD earlier that year. According to this study, approximately 450 documented homeless people resided within our city limits.

"We have a divine mandate to address the needs of those that are suffering in our community!" my boss exclaimed.

This speech excited some of the ministers present. It bored others, and I remember that it really pissed off one pastor in particular.

While the conversation seemed to be gaining momentum, our irritated colleague interrupted and through a thick southern accent akin to Ricky Bobby said,

> *"I don't know what this whole missional gobbly-gook is about but it seems to me that we just need to teach people about Jesus and all the problems in our world will naturally fix themselves. My child was home the other day and 'a homeless person' rang our doorbell and asked for some money. Well, my baby went right inside and instead of calling the Deputy Sheriff's Office, my kids decided to show 'em the love of Jesus. My baby reached in the deep freezer and got that homeless person a frozen pizza, and a can of beans from out of the cupboard. They walked back to the front door,*

looked that 'hobo' square in the eyes, gave 'em the food, and told 'em to have a blessed day."

A thunderous applause erupted in the chamber. It was clear that the children of this story had been recognized as heroes.

It was at this point that I no longer could contain myself. I started laughing so hysterically that the entire room stared at me in disgust.

"Is there something funny to you, Christopher?" the vice-chair inquired.

I was shocked that I even needed to explain why this story was so idiotic.

"Well, first of all, I think the term 'hobo' is offensive and ignores the fact that they are God's children, too. I believe the appropriate term would be 'a person experiencing homelessness.' That aside, if this person was indeed experiencing homelessness, do you think they would have had access to an oven to cook the frozen pizza? Did they have a can opener for the beans?

"Last time I checked, telling someone in need that Jesus loves them doesn't heat up your frozen food if you are living outdoors in the winter," I explained in a sarcastic tone.

I was never invited back to those meetings.

This line of thinking is common in many churches. I call it "charitable masturbation." Sure it feels good, but unless it is thought out, it doesn't provide a sense of relief to anyone else but yourself.

Though the "church plants" that I served were far from perfect, I am truly grateful for those experiences. I am not thankful for the headaches or the scars that were left by some of the pastors for whom

I worked. But I am grateful for the exposure to church planting and the clarity that this time of employment gave me in my career. By serving these churches with my talents, I found my passion: Creating new and progressive models of Christian community.

I attended many seminars that discussed the tools of the trade. I spent hours on the phone with prominent leaders in the field. I spent weeks at training camps where we shaped our mission, vision, and values to create a blueprint for our ideal communities. I read countless books on different models of emergent church communities, and with intense study and preparation through the Disciple of Christ's church planter training process, I ventured out to form my core team and build a new congregation.

But like the soda cans, cigarette butts, and plastic bags that slowly were being exposed by the rising light over the marshlands, my new horizons eventually illuminated many areas of imperfection within my own life. After years of remaining silent about these issues, it was time to reach out for help.

"The mailbox is full and cannot receive any messages at this time. Goodbye," the robotic voice informed me.

I hung up the phone and ran my fingers furiously through what was once a dense head of curly black hair. Apparently, a decade of ministry was having a negative impact on my follicular fortitude.

My breathing was quick, the dock felt as if it was spinning, and I was on the cusp of a major panic attack.

"Hey Siri. Redial," I said impatiently.

The phone rang several times, and the automated voice once again informed me that there was no space available for me to leave a voice message.

"Owen, please pick up!" I growled into my iPhone. I pressed the icon to end the call and then quickly commanded Siri to redial again. This illogical cycle continued for about thirty minutes. After what felt like the hundredth attempt, the phone rang twice and suddenly there was an exasperated breath on the other end of the line.

"Owen? Owen, is that you?" I asked desperately. "I am so sorry. I know that I have called like a million times, but Owen this can't wait,"

"Do you have any idea what time it is, Mate?" Owen groaned.

Before I gave my dear friend the chance to scold me for my rude behavior, multiple emotional explanations sailed from my lips.

"Owen, I am sorry, I just … I just didn't know who to call. I am alone right now. Honestly, I am ashamed to even be talking to you about this, but I need help. I have nowhere to go, Owen. I literally have nowhere to sleep tonight. None of our friends can take me in. I'm desperate. I just need a place to crash for a few days, and then hopefully I can figure this out. Owen, may I please stay with you?" I asked in total embarrassment.

There was a pause on the other end of the phone. Even though I could not see my friend's face, it was obvious that Owen was completely perplexed about my request.

"Did your family get evicted? Christopher, how do you have nowhere to go? I was just at your house last week," Owen said.

"The house is fine, Owen, but we are not fine. I can't stay there," I said, fighting tears.

Even though there was complete silence on the other line, I knew that Owen finally understood my situation. Yet I still felt that I needed to confess my predicament aloud. I needed to remove the burden that I had been carrying for years from my shoulders.

"Owen we ... we are getting a divorce," I admitted through weak and cracking vocal chords.

Owen took a deep breath and exhaled slowly. For a minute or two we both sat in utter silence. Then, after waiting for a response, I heard a drawer quickly open and close. The sound of a door to a backyard being opened, screaming cicadas, and the striking of a cigarette lighter. These sounds that entered my bluetooth earpiece painted a clear depiction of what Owen was doing to relieve some of the weight caused by my heavy news. After taking a long drag on a cigarette, Owen responded.

"Bring your things and come over to my place soon. We will talk more when you arrive. You can stay with me, Mate," Owen decreed.

"Thank you, Owen! Thank you so much! I did not know who else to call. I am so sorry. I know it was rude," I said, choking on my shame.

"That is what church is for, Christopher. You need help, Mate, and I told you when I agreed to join this church that I did not possess much, but that I would do what I can to help. Obviously you need help, and I am here for you. There is only one condition for you staying in my home." Owen had a knack for speaking in riddles.

"I am listening," I said curiously.

"My condition is that you are not allowed to argue about where you sleep. That is the only rule for guests in my home. If you are cool with that, Mate, then you come on over. If not, then I am sorry to say that I cannot help you," Owen mumbled through a cigarette.

"That is not going to be a problem at all Owen," I said.

"*I really hope this is not going to be a problem,*" I thought.

It was 9:30 in the morning when I arrived. I knocked on the door, and Owen opened the entrance to a small two-bedroom cottage. Everything in Owen's dwelling was compact, simplified, and yet what little furnishings and decorations were present were all adorned in bright and vivid colors. Owen was originally from an island nation outside of the U.S., and all of the decor in this living space exuded an island vibe.

A large tank, teeming with exotic fish, bubbled in the corner of the living room. Tropical plants were scattered about the home, and in the middle of the living area sat two hand-carved rocking chairs side by side.

We walked into the kitchen/pantry/dining room combo and sat down to a two-top table to have a cup of coffee and finish the conversation we had started on the phone. My friend carved us both a slice of gourmet cheesecake, and we began to unpack my predicament.

Looking back, this may have been the most *Golden Girls*-esque moment of my life.

Owen was an excellent conversationalist with a similar faith journey to my own. That is probably why we got along so well. We were both raised in ultra-conservative environments, we both recently had abandoned conservative Christianity, and we both were exploring progressive theology. We often would meet during the week to discuss our thoughts concerning process theology, open theism, and preterism. It was nice to have someone who spoke the same language in my life, and it was wonderful to have a compassionate ear that would listen to my struggles while I leaned on them for encouragement.

I started to discuss all that had been going on for years in my marriage. I told Owen how my soon-to-be ex and I had sought "Christian counseling" multiple times for years and explained how it inevitably only made things worse. None of the Christian "counselors" we used were credentialed psychologists, and all of them were practicing terrible relational dynamics themselves. I had learned the hard way that using the Bible as a road map to build a fruitful marriage in modern times is terrible advice.

As I spoke, Owen nodded periodically to let me know that my pain truly was being heard. After a few hours of conversation, Owen began to wince in pain. This discomfort wasn't caused by hearing my predicament, but was a result of an aging body. At just over fifty years old, Owen had been dealing with shoulder problems and back pain for decades. An old motorcycle injury had been the source of my friend's daily discomfort. Owen's active lifestyle and stubborn demeanor certainly didn't help.

After hours of sitting at the table, Owen's shoulder pain had become an understandable distraction. We both decided that we could pick up the conversation later. Owen worked nights and needed to sleep, and I was noticeably exhausted as well. I was instructed by Owen to try and get some rest.

I decided to take a quick shower before going to bed, because I am one of those weirdos who cannot fall asleep unless I am squeaky-clean. After I showered, I put on some pajamas and exited the teal bathroom only to see Owen standing at the end of the hall.

"Remember, Christopher, there will be no arguing about where you sleep," Owen barked.

"I remember," I said, not knowing exactly what to expect of my new living arrangement.

I had been trying to piece this puzzle together since I arrived. The guest bedroom was only furnished with a fiberboard computer desk. This space appeared to have some room for a sleeping bag on the floor. At this point I assumed that this office space would serve as my temporary bedroom. This assumption seemed especially logical, since Owen was standing directly in front of the doorway to the computer room.

It was not an ideal situation, but it was better than living out of my Prius.

My initial hypothesis would be proven to be incorrect. Owen nodded and pointed toward the master bedroom to my left.

"That is your bed, Mate," Owen stated firmly.

Owen pointed toward the only room with an actual bed in the entire home. Consequently, this also was the only piece of high-quality furniture that my friend owned. This fifty-year-old islander with chronic back and shoulder pain willingly surrendered the only mattress in the house to me: a twenty-seven-year old, who at the time was in fairly good physical condition.

"Owen, how can I …," I started to object.

"You can, you will, and you do not have a choice. Jesus would have me treat my guests with the utmost respect and put their needs above my own. So no arguing, Christopher. My house, my rules, and the only regulation here is that guests do not have the privilege to debate with me about where they will sleep. Remember?"

My mind was blown. To this day I have not been offered an act of kindness as precious as what was given to me in this humble domicile.

I went into the room, climbed into the king-size bed, and desperately tried to get some sleep. My mind was restless and, despite the fact that my body was massively fatigued, my thoughts proceeded to anxiously race through hypothetical scenarios and questions that plagued me for hours.

What will happen with my kids?
Will they one day think I abandoned them?
What will my family and friends think?
What about my career?
Am I even called to be in the ministry?

These thoughts attacked my subconscious until the unavoidable need for slumber wrestled my body into submission. Before I had an opportunity to continue calculating possible outcomes of my present tribulation, I passed out in complete exhaustion.

I awoke early the next morning to the smells and sounds of a traditional breakfast being prepared. There was southern smoked sausage being seared, eggs being soft boiled, and thick toast cut from fresh homemade bread that was browning in the oven. The aroma of this hot meal and the freshly ground coffee that was being brewed stirred me from my chambers.

We ate this delectable breakfast together while Owen and I discussed where important items were located in the house. Owen made it emphatically clear that I would be staying no matter the outcome of my marriage and no matter how long the process would take. My friend assured me that I would not be left to suffer through this process alone. Owen also refused to accept, or even discuss, any reimbursement for rent during my stay.

At one point during the meal, Owen looked down toward the table. I could see that there was some burden weighing heavy on my friend's mind. I assumed that perhaps I had already outstayed my welcome. I began to feel concerned as I saw Owen struggling to formulate words.

"There is something that I have been putting off telling you for quite some time. In my home my parents taught me that it is terrible manners to learn a friend's secret without sharing one of your own. So I guess now is as good of a time as any. I have never told anyone in this city what I am about to share at this table." Owen said while stirring a spoon through a half-empty coffee mug.

"Owen, I know that you are divorced. You told me that months ago, remember?" I asked, assuming that my friend had forgotten this conversation. This was not out of character for Owen. Like me, Owen is an incredibly forgetful soul. "I hope my presence is not causing you to relive your past traumas with divorce as well." I said as I became concerned about our newly agreed upon living arrangement.

Owen took a deep breath, looked me directly in the eyes, and said, "It is not that, Christopher. You are always welcome here. But if you stay you need to know that you are at risk.

"Christopher, I'm undocumented."

This was, without a doubt, one of the most painful parts of my life. One from which I, my children, and my ex never will completely recover. After years of both of us trying to make things work for our children, everything had fallen apart. Who would have thought that choosing to follow the relational guidelines found in a centuries old mysoginistic cannon could be harmful to a marriage?

Out of respect for my children and their mother, I do not wish to say any more on the matter regarding our past relationship. Though the dynamic with my ex can be like oil and water at times, our children are well housed, well fed, and supported in their pursuit of extracurricular activities.

Besides, this is not a story about my former marriage. It is a story about Owen.

Owen completely shifted my position on undocumented citizens. Before I had experienced living with Owen, I opposed the concept of open borders. My past objections to welcoming more foreigners as residents in America was not from religious influence, nor was it due to prejudice or xenophobia.

My opposition stemmed from an ignorant view of economics.

For years I had been taught that America was massively in debt and that our debt was caused by socialism, unions, and America's lax policies that allow undocumented citizens into the country to abuse our kindness. It would be years before I realized that the source of America's financial sandpits have always been our nation's military budget, weapons development, and corporate welfare. However, Owen is responsible for helping me understand the errors of my ways.

My experience while living with Owen caused me not only to reassess my values. Our time together proved that everything conservative Christianity had taught me about undocumented citizens was unfounded. This undocumented citizen, unlike what I was taught, had ethical ways of making money. Owen was far from a criminal, and in actuality gave money to an American relative annually for them to pay the government extra money toward the taxes that Owen would have owed if my roommate was an American citizen.

Owen paid every medical bill that came in the mail, purchased all necessary medications, and if any health care needs could not be paid in full, this hardworking individual would set up payment plans with the local hospital.

In the years that we knew each other, I never once witnessed Owen take advantage of any system.

Every stereotype I had been told about "illegals" was wrong. This undocumented individual was not freeloading. Statistically speaking, Owen paid a higher percentage of taxes than any American billionaire. This relationship helped me realize that billionaires are the real leeches of our economy. Not undocumented citizens.

Hell, Owen, with no legal obligation, willingly paid more taxes than the 45th president of the United States.

The only thing Owen and Donald Trump have in common is that neither one of them has produced a tax return. I suspect that they both have different reasons for that, but I am a pastor, not Robert Mueller.

During this season of healing (in more ways than one), I began to dive into the Scriptures and realized that not only were American stereotypes about undocumented citizens incorrect, but the conservative evangelical praxis of not welcoming the immigrant is downright heretical.

The book of Exodus says,

> *When a foreigner resides among you in your land, do not mis-*
> *treat them. The foreigner residing among you must be treated as*
> *your native-born. Love them as yourself, for you were foreigners*
> *in Egypt.*

Egypt was an imperial monstrosity that had enslaved the Jewish people. Egypt only valued the Hebrews as construction equipment. This passage in Exodus served as a reference for Jewish people to never create systems that exploit refugees and immigrants as slaves, or cheap labor. This passage was meant to serve as a reminder that the Jewish people once were systematically oppressed and Egyptian governance was a societal construct that Jewish people should never aspire to build.

But Egypt is exactly what Christians allowed the United States to become.

As I am writing this chapter, it is December 2018, and there is currently a tyrannical overlord that rose to power in the United States by hijacking the Christian faith. Despite overwhelming evidence of criminal activity, Russian collusion, racism, bigotry, sexual crimes, infidelity, and total incompetence, Trump still has the support of 87 percent of American evangelicals.

Recently, this imperial imbecile resorted to a partial government shutdown in a financial tug-of-war to acquire funds for a racist border wall. This is absurd considering most undocumented citizens arrive at ports of entry or overstay their visas. Trump even used a migrant caravan of asylum seekers to convince citizens that our country is being invaded. Yet, the president and evangelical business owners who support Trump's grotesque agenda of "Finishing the Wall" are guilty as fuck when it comes to exploiting undocumented citizens for cheap labor themselves.

I personally have debated countless hours with GOP supporters who own landscaping companies. They pay undocumented workers far less than minimum wage for back-breaking labor. These privately owned businesses profit well over six figures annually in states with incredibly low costs of living.

American agricultural corporations are even more culpable in the subjugation of innocents seeking a better life. These institutions pay undocumented workers pennies on the dollar to harvest mountains of produce across the United States that will provide sustenance to most of our nation's populace.

These amazing laborers literally put food on the tables of indignant bigots and, instead of encouraging thankfulness, evangelical rhetoric has caused conservative citizens to want to see these fieldworkers deported. This is the antithesis of the all loving God found in the Bible.

The book of Malachi states firmly that God's favor forever extends to the marginalized:

> *"So I will come to put you on trial. I will be quick to testify against sorcerers, adulterers and perjurers, against those who defraud laborers of their wages, who oppress the widows and the fatherless, and deprive the foreigners among you of justice, but do not fear me," says the Lord Almighty.*

Because of this, I believe that it is our job, in these dark times, to remind the United States of prophetic historical truths that foretell of our downfall. For that is what every oppressive system of governance does eventually. They all fall, and they fall hard. If we cannot take an unbiased examination of our past and present, and alter our current trajectory, then one day the foundation of our nation will fracture. If we continue to oppress the stranger, create victims, and promote poverty, then maybe it should.

Contrary to popular belief, God is not an American.

This means that we have to stop building border walls that further divide humanity, and start setting tables to invite all to share in our abundance. In Trump's America, many Christians would argue against this.

There is a noticeable disconnect with many professing Christians who have adopted the mantra of "Making America Great Again."

If we are honest about our nation's origins of genocide, theft, slavery, neglect, and abuse, it is clear that we have never been great.

We have been powerful.

Between these two distinctions there is an ocean of difference.

This truth may be tough to accept, but it is essential to absorb. I believe that ancient Judaism depicts a god with an agenda that will not be ignored. The God of the Bible is in the business of destroying systems of power that create a class of powerless victims. This naturally implies that tyrant kingdoms must perish if they refuse to repent. If there is one thing that the Scriptures have taught us, it is that exploitive empires like America cannot stand.

Take Sodom for example. The book of Ezekiel says,

> *Now this was the sin of your sister Sodom: She and her daughters were arrogant, overfed and unconcerned; they did not help the poor and needy.*

There is quite a bit of debate as to whether the city of Sodom even existed, or if it was metaphorical. Either way, the Bible indicates that it was not destroyed for "sexual immorality." At least not in the way that fundamentalists understand sexual immorality.

Genesis 19 says,

> *The two messengers of God came to Sodom in the evening, and Lot was sitting in the gateway of Sodom. When Lot saw them, he rose to meet them, and bowed down with his face to the ground. He said, "Please, my lords, turn aside to your servant's house and spend the night, and wash your feet; then you can rise early and go on your way." They said, "No; we will spend the night in the square." But he urged them strongly; so they turned aside to him and entered his house; and he made them a feast, and baked unleavened bread, and they ate. But before they lay down, the men of the city, the men of Sodom, both young and old, all the people to the last man, surrounded the house; and they called to Lot, "Where are the men who came to you tonight? Bring them out to us, so that we may lay with them."*

As we examine this passage, it is important to recognize the distinction between sex, and sexual assault. Carefully read the verse above again.

The citizens of Sodom did not show up at Lot's home to have an orgy with these angelic messengers. They didn't have a gift basket with wine, chocolates, lingerie, whipped cream, sex toys, and a mixtape of Boys 2 Men.

Every Sodomite that identified as male showed up to abuse these unwelcome visitors of their city in an act called "topping."

"Topping" is a horrific practice that still is used in many misogynistic cultures. This despicable crime mostly is inflicted on prisoners of war, or unwelcome strangers who identify as male. "Topping" abuses these people by treating them the same way these primitive societies treat those that identify as women. In many primeval cultures of both past and present, women are unjustly recognized as nothing more than breeding stock. They treat the men who were imprisoned the same way they treat women.

In short, "topping" is the criminal method of rape used to display social dominance over unwelcome guests and prisoners.

This practice is seen elsewhere in the Bible. We can see passages describing this act in Leviticus:

You shall not lie with a man as with a woman; it is an abomination.

Again, these Old Testament verses condemned rape and the humiliation of innocent human beings. They were not intended to regulate varying sexual identities.

Inevitably, when discussing sexuality with fundamentalists, I encounter evangelicals who refuse to talk about the Bible from a scholarly approach. These Christians only wish to discuss what they can read in the Bible for themselves. They care very little about the historical events surrounding biblical narratives and even less about the original language that inscribed these stories.

So let's take a moment to examine elements found in the English translations of the story of Sodom that remain to be incredibly precarious in a modern tongue.

Lot went out of the door to the men, shut the door after him, and said, "I beg you, my brothers, do not act so wickedly. Look, I have two daughters who have not known a man; let me bring them out to you, and do to them as you please; only do nothing to these men, for they have come under the shelter of my roof."

Lot offered innocent children to be raped in place of the angels. Who in their right mind would surrender the children to rapists to protect complete strangers? No wonder this town was destroyed.

In closing, the people of Sodom, whether this story was a metaphor or historical occurrence, were not destroyed for sexuality. This city was obliterated for establishing a cultural norm that either ignored or worsened the conditions that people were sleeping in.

The tale of Sodom is not a litmus test for our permissible sexual practices. It is not a story that defines LGBTQ people as sinners. The story of Sodom is a warning to nations that are indifferent and abusive.

(We'll discuss the topics of sex and sexuality in greater depth in chapter nine of this book titled "Centurions.")

In that knowledge, if the tale of Sodom was rewritten today I would find it hard to believe that any other nation besides the United States could be utilized to represent this city. Sadly, based on their voting record, I am positive that the GOP and their ultra-conservative evangelical minions would be cast as the Sodomites.

Especially since America's current administration is culpable for the deaths of child refugees who literally were locked in fucking cages!

———

For two years I lived with Owen. I have never encountered a person who challenged me to grow the way that Owen did. Throughout the entire painful process of my divorce, Owen was an anchor in maintaining my sanity.

I have never met another Christian who goes to the extreme lengths to help a struggling neighbor the way Owen did, including the Christian that wrote this book. I always will remember our theological conversations over coffee. I always will remember the laughter we shared. I will never forget how this person stimulated my understanding of the Gospel of Jesus in a tangible way. May Owen's story challenge and inspire all who read it. In some small way, may these pages forever memorialize the greatest example of divine compassion that I ever had the privilege of calling my friend.

EDEN

"Owen, I'm telling ya, social media is the best way to advertise our Bible study. We just have to figure out a solid marketing hook. We have to come up with a catchy phrase or a powerful logo that will cause intrigue," I said while staring intensely at the blinking cursor on my Facebook page.

The blank field on my screen mocked me for my lack of creativity. After an hour of deep contemplation, I still had no idea what marketing strategy would yield the results that I was looking for.

It was almost a year after my separation. But even after this hardship I was still in the process of forming a strong core team for a church plant. I longed for spiritual community now more than ever, and our Bible study would be a way for me to locate more like-minded individuals.

"I am drawing a blank, Mate," Owen sighed while lighting a cigarette.

"Yeah, me too," I confessed as I massaged my thumb and index finger through my soul patch.

"Well, there is no rush, Christopher. Maybe take some time and pray on it. Eventually something is bound to …"

"Holy shit! I've got it!" I interrupted as my fingers quickly left my facial hair and fiercely raced over my MacBook keyboard.

I proofread my post and chuckled at the controversy that it soon would generate. I leaned back in my chair with my hands behind my head with my soul beaming in self-content. I now was the proud parent of a marketing masterpiece.

"Buckle up!" I warned Owen as I clicked the "share" icon.

"Ha! What did you say?" giggled Owen.

"Beer and Bible Study Wednesday Nights at 7:00 p.m. Join us as for our first gathering this week as we discuss evolution and the Bible," I said while chewing on a pencil eraser and raising my eyebrows clownishly.

"Well, that is certainly a clear announcement, but why do you think we need to buckle up?" Owen questioned.

"Owen, 70 percent of my Facebook friends are evangelical Southern Baptists, PCA Presbyterians, or Pentecostals. We are smack-dab in the middle of the Bible Belt. That Facebook post could quite possibly be the most triggering collection of words that they have read in their entire lives," I laughed.

With a maniacal expression, I turned around mock-eerily in my desk chair. I slowly raised my pinky to the edge of my lip with one hand, and I pretended to pet an invisible cat in my lap with the other.

"It might even generate *one million likes*," I said, changing both the pitch and inflection of my voice to mimic Mike Myers.

For a moment I had forgotten that Owen was much older than me, and I was disappointed that my Dr. Evil impression fell flat.

"Christopher, you have managed to piss off every church you have worked for because of your liberal ideals. Do you really think that this post is going to surprise anyone? No one is going to respond to this," Owen declared while taking a long drag on a menthol.

"Really? Because the eighteen comments generated since I posted it a minute ago say otherwise," I said, pointing at the screen while basking in all that was my evil genius.

"You're shitting me!" Owen cackled, leaning in for a closer examination of the fruits of my pot stirring.

The comments ranged from insults to concern from the local evangelicals who populated my Facebook friend list. Of course the word "heresy" was thrown in once or twice (shocker!). However, I have to admit that some of these negative comments were humorous.

"Christopher, that is a great idea! Hey, ya know what? Let's do a prayer and porn night on Thursdays," one person suggested.

"Well, we know where the next Crusade should start," scoffed a local minister.

"I'd have to be drunk to listen to that evolution horseshit," said a local business owner.

I took most of these comments with a grain of salt. After all, the post had done exactly what I had intended it to do. Controversy is a wonderful tool for advertisement. Within minutes this post had sparked a lot of attention. In two hours, my advertisement had well over 150 likes and 100 comments. The vast majority of the comments were negative, but the haters didn't matter.

Based on my primitive understanding of Facebook algorithms, a post with lots of likes and comments meant that my Bible study advertisement would have a higher priority on other people's feeds. When the Facebook friends of the Beer And Bible Study naysayers saw the responses to my controversial post, they also would see the description of our event. I was sure that these Christian conservatives in my network had to have a few moderates or liberals on their friend list, and local undiscovered lefties were my target demographic.

The controversy continued to spread. After hours of online debating with local evangelicals, a few locals who were part of these conservative's social network and who had been hurt by Christianity in their past, messaged me to express interest in our meeting.

The following Wednesday night, twelve people attended our gathering at a local bar. The number of people present was a fun coincidence that Owen didn't hesitate to point out.

"Hey, wasn't there some famous Rabbi that started a movement with twelve people?" my ministry partner inquired with a wink.

Each of us enjoyed some delicious southern cuisine and a variety of Low Country craft beers before the Bible study commenced. Shrimp and grits, chicken and waffles, shrimp burgers, fried green tomatoes, fried pickles, and she-crab soup filled the table as we opened our gathering with a time of feasting and fellowship. Everything was flowing smoothly. People were connecting and everyone present seemed genuinely to be enjoying each other's company. It is a fond memory that I will always carry with me.

After our meal, we had a quick moment of prayer and we opened our Bibles to Genesis chapter one. Just before we started reading the Scriptures, a visitor spoke up with a few observations.

"So I know I might be stepping on some toes here, but y'all know this book is all bullshit, right?" our guest asked mockingly while pointing at our Bibles.

The first-time visitor teasing us about our religion was my friend Bobby.

Bobby had a degree in biology, and was also a volunteer for local environmental efforts. We knew that Bobby was a devout atheist, but we invited Bobby to join us anyway.

Those seated at our table looked to me for guidance. I could tell by the shared expression of shock on everyone's face that they were all unsure if questions, doubt, and cursing were permitted in this space.

"Well, Bobby, you and I might not agree on all spiritual matters. But we do agree on one thing. Creationism is some serious bullshit," I said as I raised my glass to our group's new charming instigator as we opened our Bibles.

◄———◄ ┣═══►

In youth, Bobby was a Christian who was devoutly involved with a large church and active in their youth program. Bobby had a rough childhood and would consistently attend church every Wednesday night to escape the troubles that awaited at home. Things were wonderful for Bobby in the youth department, and this spiritual community was a much needed space of nourishment and respite.

That all changed when the youth director spotted Bobby carrying a book about dinosaurs.

"What is that?" demanded the youth director from the stage.

"It is a book about the Mesozoic Era. The science fair is coming up, and I want to enter my project on paleontology," Bobby said proudly.

"That book is satanic! Dinosaurs are not in the Bible! Therefore, they never existed. They would have been mentioned in Genesis if God had made them. These giant lizards are a liberal conspiracy," proclaimed the pastor.

"We know they existed because paleontologists have discovered their fossils," Bobby objected sheepishly.

"Well, then, where are these dinosaurs today?" asked the youth director sarcastically.

"Some species became extinct, while others evolved into birds," Bobby stubbornly protested, unaware of the ramifications that are associated with presenting scientific fact in an ultra-conservative sanctuary.

"Evolution is not real! Those bones are a conspiracy, and that book is demonic. Fossils, or whatever you call them, were put in the dirt by the devil to test our faith," professed the minister over Bobby's small voice.

"How do you know that for sure? Were you there?" Bobby asked confrontationally.

"Bobby, I think it is best that you go home. If you can't accept that the Bible is our ultimate authority on all things in life, then perhaps it is best that you never come back. We don't need any children in this church becoming corrupted by left-wing theories and liberal agendas," the pastor declared.

Bobby was devastated and because of this painful memory Bobby has remained a steadfast and unapologetic atheist opposed to religion.

The fundamentalists in Bobby's story are the types of self-pro-claimed "Christ followers" that do the most damage to parishioners because their toxicity is well intended. Though their theology is far from wholesome, these hyper fundamentalists do not want people to burn in Hell for all eternity on their watch. In their misguided minds, they quite literally are saving people's souls.

Because of this "savior complex," misguided converts have an intol-erance to academia that is derived from a place of concern for the salvation for the "lost souls" of this world. Simply put, as infuriat-ing and naive as many evangelicals can be, they do not know any better. This, of course, is a reason for their behavior, but it is not an adequate excuse.

Regardless of how well intentioned these folks are, it does not erase their impact. Their beliefs have a horrendous effect on the scientific community, the environment, our economy, our culture, and our political system.

This is why I surmise that one of the most beneficial things pro-gressives can do is educate the masses about the origins of defective theology.

I theorize that biblical ignorance actually emanates from within the pages of our sacred writings, or at least from how we interpret them. The Bible is often read like a novel. In spite of this, it is not a single book. It is a composition of differing forms of literature, inscribed by many authors, transcribed from differing ancient lan-guages, influenced by contrasting political climates, conceived in numerous regions, intended for distinct audiences, and compiled over the span of centuries. If we read this Book of Books like a single book, then we have missed much of what was being said. I believe these ancient sages, leaders, heroes, rebels, and prophets had wisdom FOR us, but their texts certainly weren't written TO us.

There is not a single author of any book, in either testament, that knew they would be contributing to a religious canon. To read these Scriptures as if those of us residing in the present are somehow predestined recipients is massively detrimental to a contextual understanding of the Bible.

For example: Christian zealots excavate a sizable portion of their theological positions from the stories found in Genesis chapter one and Genesis chapter two. They assume these stories were written as historical narratives. The problem with this method of understanding the Scriptures is that it is hysterically FALSE!

Genesis was never meant to be taken literally.

In fact, the first two chapters of the Bible massively contradict one another.

Need proof?

There are two drastically different accounts of creation in the first two chapters of Genesis. If we recite both stories in tandem, we can easily observe that these narratives have several major discrepancies in their tellings of humanity's origin. Humanity's entire populace is spontaneously spoken into existence following animals and plants in the first chapter of Genesis.

Genesis chapter one says,

> In the beginning when God created the heavens and the earth, the earth was a formless void and darkness covered the face of the deep, while a wind from God swept over the face of the waters. Then God said, "Let there be light"; and there was light. And God saw that the light was good; and God separated the light from the darkness. God called the light Day, and the darkness he called Night. And there was evening and there was morning, the

first day. And God said, "Let there be a dome in the midst of the waters, and let it separate the waters from the waters." So God made the dome and separated the waters that were under the dome from the waters that were above the dome. And it was so. God called the dome Sky. And there was evening and there was morning, the second day. And God said, "Let the waters under the sky be gathered together into one place, and let the dry land appear." And it was so. God called the dry land Earth, and the waters that were gathered together he called Seas. And God saw that it was good. Then God said, "Let the earth put forth vegetation: plants yielding seed, and fruit trees of every kind on earth that bear fruit with the seed in it." And it was so. The earth brought forth vegetation: plants yielding seed of every kind, and trees of every kind bearing fruit with the seed in it. And God saw that it was good. And there was evening and there was morning, the third day. And God said, "Let there be lights in the dome of the sky to separate the day from the night; and let them be for signs and for seasons and for days and years, and let them be lights in the dome of the sky to give light upon the earth." And it was so. God made the two great lights—the greater light to rule the day and the lesser light to rule the night—and the stars. God set them in the dome of the sky to give light upon the earth, to rule over the day and over the night, and to separate the light from the darkness. And God saw that it was good. And there was evening and there was morning, the fourth day.

And God said, "Let the waters bring forth swarms of living creatures, and let birds fly above the earth across the dome of the sky." So God created the great sea monsters and every living creature that moves, of every kind, with which the waters swarm, and every winged bird of every kind. And God saw that it was good. God blessed them, saying, "Be fruitful and multiply and fill the waters in the seas, and let birds multiply on the earth." And there was evening and there was morning, the fifth day. And God said, "Let the earth bring forth living creatures of every kind: cattle and creeping things and wild animals of the earth of every kind." And it was so. God made the wild animals of the earth of every kind, and the cattle of every kind, and everything that creeps upon the ground of every kind. And God saw that it was good. Then God said, "Let us make humankind in our image, according to our likeness; and let them have dominion over the fish of the sea, and over the birds of the air, and over the cattle, and over all the wild animals of the earth, and over every creeping thing that creeps upon the earth."

So God created humankind in his image,
in the image of God he created them;
male and female he created them.

God blessed them, and God said to them, "Be fruitful and multiply, and fill the earth and subdue it; and have dominion over the fish of the sea and over the birds of the air and over every living thing that moves upon the earth." God said, "See, I have given you every plant yielding seed that is upon the face of all the earth, and every tree with seed in its fruit; you shall have them for food. And to every beast of the earth, and to every bird of the air, and to everything that creeps on the earth, everything that has the breath of life, I have given every green plant for food." And it was so. God saw everything that he had made, and indeed, it was very good. And there was evening and there was morning, the sixth day.

However, in the second chapter of Genesis, Adam is solely sculpted from the earth before plants and animals were created. Eve is not mentioned until after the creation narrative at a later time. The second chapter of Genesis says,

In the day that the Lord God made the earth and the heavens, when no plant of the field was yet in the earth and no herb of the field had yet sprung up—for the Lord God had not caused it to rain upon the earth, and there was no one to till the ground; but

a stream would rise from the earth, and water the whole face of the ground— then the Lord God formed man from the dust of the ground, and breathed into his nostrils the breath of life; and the man became a living being. And the Lord God planted a garden in Eden, in the east; and there he put the man whom he had formed. Out of the ground the Lord God made to grow every tree that is pleasant to the sight and good for food, the tree of life also in the midst of the garden, and the tree of the knowledge of good and evil.

Hence, we cannot logically conclude that the Bible should be read as an inerrant document when there is a blatant contradiction exposed after reading the first two chapters.

Contrary to what many fundamentalists believe, a contextual understanding of Genesis would be that it originally was an ancient oral tradition bursting with poetic metaphor. It was not a historical textbook. The first eleven chapters of Genesis are not a centuries-old rendition of *On the Origin of Species,* Genesis is not a scientific dissertation on astronomy, and it does not contain journal entries written by the survivors of an apocalyptic flood. It is an allegory. It never was intended to be read literally. In many ways, the first eleven chapters of Genesis were a political statement.

The authors of Genesis wanted to make a public contrast between their tribal deity, and the gods of the Babylonian empire. Ancient Semitics took Babylonian myths of creation that had been in circulation for generations, and used them as a framework to communicate the profound differences between the characteristics of their god and the pantheon of the Babylonians. The result of repurposing Babylonian mythos was a strikingly similar legend with interesting and extremely noticeable alterations.

In the Babylonian creation poem, their idols were a cruel assortment of menacing beings. They toyed with humanity and used them as disposable pawns for their own amusement and for their own benefit. In the Jewish rendition of creation there was only one god, and that divine spirit was named Elohim. The word "Elohim" is,

Male and female,
singular and plural,
a verb and a noun.

With this loaded word, the authors of the creation poems basically were saying that their god, unlike the Babylonian gods, is beyond comprehension. In the Hebrew version of creation, God did not wish to abuse humanity, but rather wished to invite humans to become Elohim's co-creators of paradise on Earth and stewards of the environment.

(This is why denying the catastrophic effects of climate change is a deeply spiritual failing that has long deserved our attention and repentance.)

The ancient Hebrews constructed this alternate story of creation as a way to give a holy middle finger to the empire of Babylon. The opening chapters of Genesis were a manifesto against the primary source of their oppression. This is why believing that Genesis is an origin story misses thematic messages that are far more meaningful, logical, and applicable today.

Regrettably, the way fundamentalists read the book of Genesis affects more areas of our existence than just conservation and ecology.

Biblical literalists extract their criteria for sexual ethics from two of the primary characters within the Genesis creation poem. In the mind of an evangelical, sex is restricted between a cisgendered man and woman. In their eyes, according to the first book of the Bible, God created Adam and Eve for a divine reason. One of the quotes that many bigoted putrid pastors will regurgitate in regard to their erroneous position on LGBTQ marital rights is that,

"God made Adam and Eve, not Adam and Steve."

It is a horrible phrase that I am sure many of you are quite familiar with.

(We'll discuss the topics of sex and sexuality in greater depth in chapter nine of this book titled "Centurions.")

In this knowledge, it is tragic that so much of Genesis is being wielded for reasons that its authors were not even remotely attempting to address. If we in the Church have a commitment to take the Scriptures seriously, then it is counterproductive to read them all literally. Conservative Christians must come to understand that just because these differing analogies of creation didn't literally occur, doesn't mean that this poetry is devoid of truth.

The fact remains that large chunks of biblical passages were either intentional allegory, or an ancient tribe documenting their limited comprehension of the mechanics of microbiology and the universe.

For example: If I were to ask anyone in America today, "Why is the sky blue?" They would go to Google on their smartphones and, after an effortless amount of research, they could explain that when light enters the Earth's atmosphere from the sun, the color blue is scattered more efficiently than other colors on the spectrum.

If you were to ask a Judaic nomadic tribal member from thousands of years ago this same question, they would have explained their belief of cosmic waters that separated the sky and ocean at the dawn of time. For them, the sky was blue because it was literally water. They envisioned Earth like a snow globe with a massive continent that was located in the center of a transparent dome. That globe was surrounded by water in every possible direction as if it were entirely submerged in an aquatic abyss. Even their concept of precipitation was primitive.

They assumed that rain descended on Earth when this "dome" opened its invisible "floodgates." They believed that these "floodgates" allowed water from the cosmic sky ocean, aka heavens, to fall on our land.

They believed that earthquakes and storms came from a gargantuan demonic serpent that lived in the cosmic sky ocean that they eventually named "the firmament." This giant serpentine demon was known as Leviathan. Leviathan would swim around the firmament and torment humanity by intentionally crashing into mountainous pillars they called the "foundations of the earth."

They also believed that the Earth was at the center of the heavens, and in the Old Testament we can see that they assumed that the sun revolved around the earth.

Today, any grade-school-level textbook can reveal that these beliefs are scientifically inaccurate. Yet, this primal understanding of the universe that is apparent in the Bible should not deter us from drawing timeless wisdom from these texts. There are moral messages of love, conservation, and justice pulsing between the covers of this ancient codex.

The book of Revelation is to be read in a similar fashion to the creation poem. Revelation also is a metaphor. It is not a book forecasting a coming apocalypse. Revelation was written as a Greek play. Theatrics with fantastical imagery were often used to make political points during the time of Christ. This final chapter of scripture was prophetic, but only in the sense that it predicted a coming collapse of both the Roman Empire and a corrupted temple system.

Both of these events did in fact happen. Revelation was a political denouncement wrapped in fantastical symbolism.

When I unpack this information regarding Genesis and Revelation that is deliberately undisclosed to evangelicals, I often get multiple objections. I take that opportunity to remind my opponents that even the staunchest conservative reads portions of the Bible as metaphor.

What parts am I referencing?

The parables of Jesus.

Parables were not unique to Jesus. This educational tool brandished by rabbis thrived long before and well after the time of Jesus. This method of storytelling was common in the rabbinic tradition. Parables were fictional stories made up by rabbis to reveal deeper moral truths about life. This style of education was applied throughout the Bible, and is apparent in other texts outside of the Gospels as well. Books like Genesis and Revelation simply are honoring the rabbinic tradition in using fiction to state their perception of morality.

No one reads the parable sections of the Gospels literally, nor should they. Does that mean that we should throw out the Scriptures because they are not literally true?

Absolutely not!

It simply means that we have to start appreciating the array of artistry that shaped the intended sentiment of each book in the Scriptures.

We must admit that our Bible is an archive. Within this archive is letters, songs, poetry, pornography, parables, prophecy, epics, metaphors, lineage, proverbs, and commandments. Once we can accept that the Bible is so much more than a singular book, we will begin to understand the dormant wisdom and hidden messages residing in its pages. When we can welcome the reality of the Christian canon being filled with various styles of literature, we can begin curing the cancer that is Christian fundamentalism. Not before.

This may be intimidating to some adherents of the faith. It will require more complexity in the process of interpreting scripture, but extra effort should be necessary when extrapolating this sacred text. If we actively are using these spiritual documents to shape our entire lifestyle, and if we see the holy writ as a source to define our modern-day communal principles, then I would argue that disciplined research is essential. By committing to a scholarly approach to the Bible that examines the language, history, genre, and political climate surrounding each book, we will not diminish the message of the Bible. This practice inevitably will enhance our theological comprehension in a far more meaningful way while also leaving little room for bigotry to endure in American pulpits.

———◄ ►———

I'd like to tell you that our Beer and Bible Study led Bobby to a fresh encounter with the Divine Mystery I call "God," but I cannot.

I'd like to tell you that I know what has happened to Bobby, but I do not.

Our conversation was not a dialogue that spurred an instant religious transformation. It didn't leave Bobby with some internal conviction that there must be something more to the human experience. If I am being honest, this scientific discussion over beer and Bibles did not even encourage Bobby to return on a weekly basis.

What it did leave Bobby with, though, was a good impression.

For the first time in decades Bobby did not feel judged by a minister or by a group of Christians for adhering to atheism. For the first time in Bobby's life, there was an orthodoxy being presented that was encouraging spiritual people to embrace scientific truth. We didn't change Bobby's mind about God, but we did alter Bobby's perception about the Christian faith.

Bobby is not alone. There are countless innocents in the scientific community bearing sizable scars from their time in "Christian" fellowship, and there is likely no singular conversation that will convert any of them back to Christianity.

In truth, they may never convert, and I would argue that this is okay.

Our dialogue with Bobby was eye-opening for me, because it revealed what so many people are yearning to see from the Church. They are begging to see scientific truth spoken to those brainwashed by fanaticism and pseudoscience. So many congregants are ensnared by absurd beliefs, and this entrapment has caused severe delays in political initiatives, worsened our global overpopulation problem, encouraged the presence of preventable disease, and hindered our ability to reverse a major oncoming climate crisis.

I may not have been able to successfully alter Bobby's views of spirituality, but Bobby's story should dictate an alternative approach in how we construct and conduct our sacred gatherings.

Meaning, it is time for churches to accept the axiom of evolution in more ways than one.

CAPTIVES

Our core team that emerged from our Beer and Bible Study began to meet every Sunday night to have dinner and explore different models that we could utilize for planting a new type of church in the twenty-first century.

After one month of deliberation we settled on creating a space that was incredibly low maintenance with virtually zero overhead. This bare-bones approach made sense for our community considering I was the only staff member, and my pastoral role most likely would be an unpaid position for the foreseeable future. We decided that our church model would require all of our core team members to tithe 10 percent of our income. However, unlike most churches, 100 percent of our donations would be allocated to purchasing groceries for us to prepare high-quality, family-style banquets every Sunday. We then would take the food that we cooked, dozens of paperback Bibles, sports gear, and a small sound system down to a city park that was located in the middle of our town's poorest district. The park had a covered picnic area with Oktoberfest tables that could seat up to eighty people comfortably. There even was access for free electricity from a power box near the picnic area into which we could plug our sound system.

This was the cathedral we constructed for our worship service.

Every week we would bring our portable sanctuary to the park. We would sing a few songs, do a discussion-based Bible study, and share communion together. After a few months of gathering, many locals came for worship and to partake in a free lunch. The aroma of delicious southern home-cooked dishes—red-skinned mashed potatoes and sawmill gravy, honey butter biscuits, bacon-wrapped meatloaf, beef stew, dirty rice, chicken gumbo, homemade mac and cheese,

BBQ pork roast, mustard greens, black-eyed peas, cornbread, fried chicken, and oxtail—filled this public space every Sunday afternoon. We decided that attendance would not be a requirement to enjoy our free meal. All were welcome at our tables to share hearty food and wonderful fellowship, including those that opted out of the liturgical portion of our weekly event. After we finished our meal, we would build relationships with the community and play football or basketball with the kids that joined us for lunch.

After we concluded the event, we would pack up our leftovers in foil-covered paper plates. Then we would personally deliver them to locals who were in need of a meal, but unable to join us at the park.

Eventually, after months of gathering, we heard about a particular homebound individual who possibly needed our help. One of our core members worked for the post office and noticed a rundown home on their route that caused them to have serious concerns for anyone who lived there. So that Sunday, Owen and I packed up some food after church and traveled to this home to see if assistance was required.

Owen and I pulled into the dirt driveway and we were instantly shocked to discover that someone could live in what appeared to be an abandoned shack. This tiny shelter sat as a beacon of abject poverty in our city. It was a shocking sight from yard to chimney.

The house rested on an ocean of dead grass and was surrounded by a minefield of mole hills and fire ant mounds that were guarding the front door. The siding was layered in dead blue paint that was noticeably peeling away from the exterior. These walls were in need of repair far greater than that of a fresh coat. One window had been replaced with what appeared to be a trash bag, and most of the window screens were torn from their frames and flapped freely in the breeze. The shack sported a rusted tin roof as a crown that could give someone tetanus just by looking at it.

Owen and I looked at each other in complete disbelief. We reached in the back seat for a ration of foiled leftovers, gave each other a nod of encouragement, and headed to the front door. We walked up to the porch, dodging several rotting steps along the way, and rang the doorbell.

I was not surprised that the doorbell no longer was functional, but before we had the opportunity to knock we heard a voice.

"The hell is that?' the gravelly voice growled from the other side of the door.

"My name is Christopher. Not sure if you have heard about us, but we do church in the park every Sunday. Some folks in the community suggested that we come here today. We have some homemade food with us and I was wondering if you wanted a free meal? If you are not interested, that is okay. We just thought that we would check in," I said, seeking consent.

There was a long pause of silence.

"Just leave it on the porch," the mysterious voice directed.

"Okay. No problem at all. We do this every week, so would you like me to make you a plate and bring you one on a regular basis?" I inquired.

"I guess that'd be fine, but I am way too busy for church or God right now," the gravelly voice proclaimed.

"That's okay, we just want to help when and where we can. See ya next week and have a good one, my friend," I said, hopping down from the porch. At the last second I spun back toward the door. "I almost forgot. What is your name, if ya don't mind me asking?" I probed.

"Jackson," the voice replied as a weathered hand reached from the door and took the plate of leftovers inside.

Owen and I went to Jackson's home every week, and every week we were instructed to leave our foiled meals on the porch. I tried to make conversation when I announced our arrival with Jackson. Unfortunately, I only received short answers from our secretive friend. This was fine with me, but deep down I truly was curious about this enigma known as Jackson. I desperately wanted us to meet on the same side of the porch at least once, but every Sunday we would only catch a quick glimpse of Jackson's arm retrieving the plate of food we left by the door.

Jackson was like a real-life version of Wilson from *Home Improvement,* and our limited understanding of our new friend continued for months.

But by happenstance, I was invited inside one day.

That Sunday was just like all the others. Once again I made my way up the porch and knocked on the door, but this time the mysterious voice from behind the door asked me to come inside.

I was ecstatic!

I gently opened the door and was immediately shocked at the unsanitary conditions of this living space.

The smell of fecal matter, mold, and decay smothered the room. It was impossible for me to comprehend that anyone could even survive in these conditions, much less live.

A tarnished and shadeless lamp that sat in the middle of the wooden floor illuminated the ice-cold room. A vintage television set with foiled rabbit ears in the corner fuzzed in and out of clarity. In the kitchen several wooden planks on the floor were beginning to cave in. The hallway that led to the bathroom had several small sheets of plywood scattered over multiple rotting sections of flooring.

To my right, there was a twin bed. Buried under a soiled quilted comforter and a pile of dirty laundry was the source of the mysterious voice that I had been eager to meet for months. There was my friend, lying in filth and attempting to smile through a swollen jaw.

I had finally gained the knowledge of what this entity looked like. Jackson was an elderly person of color with wild, unkempt hair, dark blue eyes, and small freckles around the nose that gave this elderly individual a beautiful childlike vibrancy. I was happy to finally see the mysterious Mr. Jackson, but at this point I was far more concerned about my friend's health.

"Are you okay? Do you need me to call a doctor or an ambulance?" I asked, shocked at the sight of Jackson's swollen jaw.

"I'm fine. I'm fine. I just got back from the doctor's office this morning. They gave me some antibiotics for my infected teeth," Jackson said, pointing at the pill bottle on the nightstand.

Jackson smiled and gestured for me to come closer.

"Thank you so much for the food. I really have been appreciating it. I am sorry that I haven't been more hospitable, but I like to keep to myself," Jackson said apologetically.

"No need to explain, buddy. I like to keep to myself, too," I said smiling.

"Pastor Christopher, I need a favor. Would you pray for me? My visit to the emergency room last night shook me up quite a bit," Jackson said weakly.

"Of course I will pray with you. Please call me Christopher. My friends call me Christopher, and we are definitely friends. 'Pastor' is just my job, not my name. I will add you to our prayer email as soon as I get home." I said as I gently patted Jackson's frail shoulder.

"No, Pastor Christopher. I mean, will you pray for me right now?" Jackson desperately pleaded.

"Of course," I said.

As we prayed, Jackson expressed a desire for life to stop being so difficult. We prayed for deliverance both financial and physical. Though I did not say this to Jackson, I knew that prayer alone was insufficient. Thoughts and prayers don't fix something like this. Initiative does.

It was then in my frustration with the notion of leaving Jackson's dire situation in the hands of God alone, that I became enlightened about the nature of prayer. Prayer does not alter unfortunate circumstances for us. Prayer endows us with the courage and insight to change the world around us. I was asking for a miracle from the Divine with Jackson, but I knew that our small church had the potential to be the miracle for which Jackson was praying.

Our prayer session and my epiphany was unintentionally interrupted by a knock at the door. A nurse who lived in the neighborhood was making a routine stop to check on Jackson. I bid farewell to them both and walked out of the house. I jumped in my Prius and was bombarded with questions from Owen concerning the details of my encounter.

I told Owen everything, including my breakthrough during the prayer session. We both knew what we had to do.

As I left Jackson's property and turned down the street, I had another eye-opening realization. Extreme poverty was not isolated to one home in my community. It was a local epidemic. This area was riddled with homes that were barely standing, and an overwhelming number of these residents were people of color.

That day Jackson had both deepened my understanding of prayer and exposed my white privilege. I had often heard the phrase "white privilege" before, but being from a blue-collar family of Irish decent, I assumed that it could not exist. After all, at the time I too believed that I had grown up "poor." Poverty and I were old acquaintances. But after experiencing Jackson's living situation, I admit that there was substantial privilege within the parameters of what I had previously considered to be "the struggle."

The poverty that I knew was nowhere near the level of the poverty I now witnessed. But my own selfishness and ego had caused me to ignore the plight of the marginalized the entirety of my life. Literally every single town that I had ever resided in had similar neighborhoods of crippling hardship, and all of these precincts were almost completely occupied by people of color.

But the white privilege that I had unwillingly procured and willfully denied for years was now undeniably staring me down through the eyes of shattered window panes and broken doorways.

That night, we gathered for consultation with our core team. I told them about the state of Jackson's home. After taking an inventory of the resources and talents available in the group, we realized that the ingredients for an answer to Jackson's prayer were seated around our table. I was an experienced painter. Owen was a talented carpenter, and in the room were multiple engineers, landscapers, and mechanics. If we could combine our resources to raise funds for materials and if we volunteered our skills, then we could completely repair Jackson's home together.

We were in unanimous agreement that something had to be done. We knew that we could make a difference, and that we should at least attempt to do so. We collectively had decided that we were done simply praying for miracles. We were ready to be a living miracle.

———◆ ▶——

One of the most troublesome passages that I have come across in the New Testament alters the way we understand the character of Jesus. The seventh chapter of Mark is hard to digest because Jesus might not have been as "perfect" as evangelical theology led us to believe.

> From there he set out and went away to the region of Tyre. He entered a house and did not want anyone to know he was there. Yet he could not escape notice, but a woman whose little daughter had an unclean spirit immediately heard about him, and she came and bowed down at his feet. Now the woman was a Gentile, of Syrophoenician origin. She begged him to cast the demon out of her daughter. He said to her, "Let the children be fed first, for it is not fair to take the children's food and throw it to the dogs." But she answered him, "Sir, even the dogs under the table eat the children's crumbs." Then he said to her, "For saying that, you may go—the demon has left your daughter." So she went home, found the child lying on the bed, and the demon gone.

If we are being honest, Jesus doesn't appear to be flawless in this encounter. Based on the conversation that we see taking place, it would appear as though Jesus is not only being confrontational to the Syrophoenician, but also exposing an internalized prejudice that Jesus had against Gentiles.

The pejorative insult "dog" frequently is employed in ancient Israel's literature, and it is one of the most crude ancient insults one could exploit to verbally assault someone within that culture.

The phrase most frequently utilized for a "dog" in the New Testament comes from the Koine Greek word *kuon.* If we were looking for a modern-day equivalent to the brash nature of this unpleasantry, we comparatively could use the term "filthy bitch."

Kuons were packs of wild dogs that roamed the streets or resided in urban dump sites. A *kuon* was not a domesticated pet, but a wild and aggressive scavenger. They were vicious, flea ridden, and diseased creatures in the eyes of locals, and these wild "dogs" were considered to be unclean according to the ancient Judaic customs of that time.

Although most verses of New Testament scripture use the word *kuon* to offend someone, it was not the chosen adage penned in the passage of Mark about the Syrophoenician.

In this text the variant *kunara* was inscribed. *Kunara* is the Koine Greek term for a household "dog." Unlike the *kuon,* these animals were domesticated. A *kunara,* was an ideal pet that was beloved by its family. During meals you would often find these pet dogs feasting near the children's table. These animals were not much different than a pet canine today, but let's not mince words here.

If I were a millionaire, I'd wager my entire fortune against a single dollar that calling an individual a "house bitch," instead of a "trashy bitch," would hardly be any less offensive to them.

Wouldn't you agree?

Even though the term *kunara* was more palatable than the pejorative *kuon* this statement from Jesus was clearly intended to aggrieve the Syrophoenician recipient.

In this knowledge, there really are only two sensible approaches in interpreting this troubling pericope. Both possibilities are based in a fair amount of assumption concerning Christ's intent. Nonetheless, I think you will find one of these two possibilities to be a far more logical interpretation than the other. Let's start with the least likely interpretation.

The first possibility is difficult to advocate. Many evangelicals assume that Christ was just joking with this Gentile. However, based on the knowledge about the harmful nature of the term "dog," it would indicate that at minimum Jesus would have been using harmful language in jest to bully someone. Frankly, I do not think crude humor that borders on the line of abusive language matches the qualities of Jesus that are depicted in the Gospels.

Make no mistake, Jesus was not always kind to folks, but Christ's insults consistently were hurled at the powerful. Jesus punched up. Never down.

This is why the second alternative to Christ's actions in this passage is the one that is the most logical. It may be hard to accept, but I believe that Christ was openly being repugnant and prejudiced toward this person. This biased behavior from Jesus was likely due to the fact that the individual requesting healing from Jesus was a Gentile.

At this time, Gentiles were considered by many ancient Jewish leaders to be unworthy of any amount of respect. Gentiles were pagans and in the eyes of ancient Judaism their cultural practices, beliefs, and norms were sinful and obscure.

In Christ's defense, the sad reality of prejudice at this point in history was not exclusive to rabbis. Gentiles equally were bigoted against Jewish folks as well. In truth, if we were to measure the cruelty of both parties, Gentiles easily would have been the greater offender.

If we observe the chronicle of events that shaped the quarrelsome dynamic between these two communities, we can understand the root of their cyclical tension.

The Jewish people had been conquered for quite some time, and their lands were colonized by Roman Gentiles. Consecutively, this meant that the Roman occupation oppressed Jewish residents. Gentiles had all the economic power and social prowess in this region.

Meaning, Gentiles were the people of privilege in Christ's day.

Now to be fair, hardships against the Jewish people were of no fault to this particular Syrophoenician, but that does not negate the historical tension and complexity that existed between these two peoples.

Conflict would be mostly unavoidable in this scenario. Regardless of whether one's ancestry originated in the conqueror, or the conquered.

Most rabbis at this time simply wanted these invaders to be put to the sword. Yet, even though the revolution that Jesus had in mind was radical, it was not violent. Be that as it may, it did not mean that Jesus would have remotely appreciated the company of a colonizer.

The ongoing hostility between Jews and Gentiles implies that Jesus may have been responding the way most rabbis would have responded to a request from any Roman Gentile. Perhaps Jesus was extending more grace than many Jewish leaders would have if they were in the same situation.

To give credit where it is due, Jesus did give assurance to the Syrophoenician that after justice came to Christ's own people, it would eventually spill over to the Gentile occupiers.

So when Jesus told the Syrophoenician that the work of this restorative movement was for the Jewish people first and the Gentile second, it was not unlike nationalistic Republican Christians reciting harmful slogans such as "America First."

But once again the Scriptures glorify another heretic-hero in this passage, and this time it is not Jesus.

Not only does our underdog identify as a woman, but our hero is a pagan. The Syrophoenician citizen stands firm in the face of these insults. Then this unnamed pagan citizen wields Jesus' own logic to launch a verbal counterattack that pointed out Jesus' hypocrisy.

Perhaps the Syrophoenician was saying something like this,

"Jesus, you call me a 'pet dog' to demean me, but even a dog's needs are provided for by loving owners. Jesus, do you lack the moral integrity to care for a pet dog in your own home? Is this the way of the 'Great Messiah?' We have all heard so much about your great leadership, but are you not even a decent enough human being that you would refuse to feed a starving family dog? Pshhh! Some Messiah you are!"

I believe that the Syrophoenician in essence questioned Christ's moral character, and possibly insinuated that Jesus may not be fit to lead a radical movement for change if Jesus' prejudice would not change.

This is where things get interesting.

This pointed statement didn't enrage Jesus. It did not make Christ defensive. It immediately caused Jesus to examine internalized racial bias that had gone unnoticed by this sacred revolutionary. These harsh words put Christ, the Messiah, in check.

I think that it is possible that Jesus received deliverance from prejudice directly from a pissed-off pagan.

I believe the idea of Jesus getting "burned" in this text is incontestable. Especially if we dissect the location of this story in the book of Mark.

The story of the Syrophoenician happens between both feedings of the multitudes in Mark. The first feeding of multitudes is listed in chapter six just before Jesus first encountered the Syrophoenician.

> The apostles gathered around Jesus, and told him all that they had done and taught. He said to them, "Come away to a deserted place all by yourselves and rest a while." For many were coming and going, and they had no leisure even to eat. And they went away in the boat to a deserted place by themselves. Many saw them going and recognized them, and they hurried there on foot from all the towns and arrived ahead of them. As he went ashore, he saw a great crowd; and he had compassion for them, because they were like sheep without a shepherd; and he began to teach them many things. When it grew late, his disciples came to him and said, "This is a deserted place, and the hour is now very late; send them away so that they may go into the surrounding country and villages and buy something for themselves to eat." But he answered them, "You give them something to eat." They said to him, "Are we to go and buy two hundred denarii worth of bread, and give it to them to eat?" And he said to them, "How many loaves have you? Go and see." When they had found out, they said,

"Five, and two fish." Then he ordered them to get all the people to sit down in groups on the green grass. So they sat down in groups of hundreds and of fifties. Taking the five loaves and the two fish, he looked up to heaven, and blessed and broke the loaves, and gave them to his disciples to set before the people; and he divided the two fish among them all. And all ate and were filled; and they took up twelve baskets full of broken pieces and of the fish. Those who had eaten the loaves numbered five thousand men.

Whether this miraculous feeding actually happened or not is still up for debate, but what is most intriguing about this story is the specific numbers that were used within both feeding of multitudes in Mark. In ancient Judaic stories different numbers had special meanings. Any time there are specific numerics used in the Bible, it is to communicate a specific point.

The sums within these two tales had very different metaphorical intentions.

In the first feeding that is depicted above, there were five fish brought to Jesus. These five fish represented the first five books of the Old Testament. Anytime the number five is utilized in the Bible, there is a good chance that it may be referencing the Torah.

Also notice that there were twelve baskets of food left over. The number twelve signifies the twelve tribes of Israel that were founded in the Torah. The number twelve was critical for the Gospels in order for them to claim Christ as the Messiah. Most scholars agree that the number twelve being utilized here is the Gospel of Mark's way of saying that Jesus was the Messiah and Christ would redeem the twelve tribes of Israel and unify them to reclaim their land from Rome. The Judaic significance of the number twelve is also why Jesus picked twelve disciples.

In short, the sixth chapter of Mark really wants us to know that Jesus is the Messiah sent to redeem the Jewish people.

Now let's leapfrog over the passages about the Syrophoenician to the following chapter in Mark to read the second feeding of multitudes. The second feeding of multitudes has almost the exact pattern of Mark chapter six, but in this account the numbers of baskets and fish in the story were altered.

The eight chapter of Mark says,

> *During those days another large crowd gathered. Since they had nothing to eat, Jesus called his disciples to him and said, "I have compassion for these people; they have already been with me three days and have nothing to eat. If I send them home hungry, they will collapse on the way, because some of them have come a long distance."*
>
> *His disciples answered, "But where in this remote place can anyone get enough bread to feed them?"*
>
> *"How many loaves do you have?" Jesus asked.*
>
> *"Seven," they replied.*
>
> *He told the crowd to sit down on the ground. When he had taken the seven loaves and given thanks, he broke them and gave them to his disciples to distribute to the people, and they did so. They had a few small fish as well; he gave thanks for them also and told the disciples to distribute them. The people ate and were satisfied. Afterward the disciples picked up seven basketfuls of broken pieces that were left over. About four thousand were present. After he had sent them away, he got into the boat with his disciples and went to the region of Dalmanutha.*

There were seven loaves in this account, not five. There were seven baskets left over, not twelve. What did the number seven mean to Jewish folks? It was a powerful number that signified God's blessing and completion. However, as important as the number seven was to Jewish people, its usage was even more significant to Gentiles. The number seven could have been a symbolic reference to the Seven Sages. These sages lived in sixth century B.C. Greece, and their philosophical writings still were respected by Romans during the time of Christ. Also, many Greek and Roman philosophers believed that the number seven was a numerical symbol of humanity's destined union to the Gods.

Other than the differing numbers used, there is one other major differentiation between the feeding of the five thousand in Mark chapter six, and the feeding of the four thousand in Mark chapter eight. This distinction may very well indicate that the second story of multitudes was Mark's way of welcoming Gentiles into the church.

Jesus was only criticized by the Pharisees in the telling of one feeding of multitudes.

Guess which one ...

The second feeding, which was an inclusive statement to the Gentile community.

My speculation is that this shift in mathematical metaphors is indicative of Jesus' transformation. A transformation that occurred after Christ was challenged by the Syrophoenician for being prejudiced. Because of our heretic hero, God's movement for justice would no longer be exclusive to one culture. It would now encompass both Jewish and Gentile communities. These stories illustrate that Jesus would come to desire the unification and equality of all peoples.

So let's recap.

First, the Gospel of Mark metaphorically states in chapter six with the original feeding of multitudes that Jesus is on a mission to benefit Jewish folks first and foremost.

Then in chapter seven Jesus encounters the Syrophoenician. Jesus reiterates an exclusive ideology and is called out by the pagan Syrophoenician for being biased. This clapback causes Jesus to question the direction of Christ's new movement.

When we get to the eighth chapter of Mark, we see a feeding of multitudes that has the exact layout as the original story, only this time the numbers utilized in the second account are a symbolic appeal for Gentiles to now be welcomed into the radical movement against the Roman Empire.

This might be a tough pill for many Christians to swallow, because it means that Christ wasn't perfect.

Should Jesus' prejudice concerning Gentiles cause us to conclude that the teaching of Jesus is unworthy of worship or respect?

NO!

First of all, the Syrophoenician was part of a culture that oppressed Christ. It does not justify Christ's animosity toward them, but it certainly makes the basis for this rivalry more comprehensible.

Let's use a modern example that many people can understand to see where Jesus was coming from:

Many Native American folks have a hard time trusting anyone who is white. Not because all white people are bad individuals, but because most of our white ancestors, at some point, were racist assholes. In the same vein, some LGBTQ folks don't initially trust people who identify as straight. They are especially cautious around straight Christians because of the harmful experiences they accrued or perceive from this demographic. Also, I personally know very few people who identify as women who initially trust folks that identify as men when they first meet them.

If you do not believe that is true, then I invite you to ask someone who identifies as a woman why that is. My book is not going anywhere. Take a break and ask them right now.

My point is that a history of pain and oppression usually yields some form of caution and/or prejudice in any society. Though this may not be a good excuse for Jesus' initial response, it is certainly a valid reason.

Now I will admit that Christ went beyond being cautious and chose to use language that was abusive, but I still admire Jesus in these passages. To me, what makes Christ's actions worthy of respect was the ability to immediately recognize and address internalized prejudices the moment it was exposed.

No excuses.

No deep thought.

No debate.

Just an instantaneous alteration in course of action.

Christ did what almost every Conservative American Christian is incapable of doing. Christ repented for harmful social behaviors.

Christ may not have epitomized perfection, but Christ exuded goodness, and that gives me hope. If the Messiah, of all people, had to address racial bias, it means we all should take pause and excavate our own internal prejudices. Even if our prejudices within our unjust society are exposed, we can acknowledge these flaws, alter our course, and move forward together on a mission to dismantle systemic inequity. However, if we truly are going to stand against systemic oppression the way that Christ did, then at some point white Christians are going to have to acknowledge our white privilege as well. By refusing to identify a causality of tyranny, we unintentionally ensure tyrannical rule's continued existence, and ultimately prolong its extraction. Yet, many white Christians refuse to acknowledge white supremacy, even though church history is saturated with racism and whitewashing. I would even go as far as to say that Jesus was killed by white supremacy.

Humor me.

Rome began as a white nation that believed their culture (not their race) was superior to the rest of the known world. They used this arrogance to fuel their conquest of dominance. Then Rome forced defeated regions to bend the knee, and adopt their culture. If they refused, these conquered citizens would be slaughtered like animals. If these regions chose to surrender to Roman authority, they would be assimilated into the empire.

It is true that over time, as a result of countless military campaigns, Rome became racially diverse. But their diversity does not change the fact that this republic began as a coalition of white people that sent their armies to force neighboring regions into cultural submission.

Enter Jesus

Jesus was in conflict with the Roman imperialist system that had oppressed Jews for generations. Jesus stood up to the rule of Caesar, was publicly executed for subversion, and despite this Rabbi's tragic death, somehow the movement of the early church did not die. Followers that emerged from the shadow of Christ's crucifixion took on the mantle of dismantling Rome. Against all odds, they began to succeed in removing the influence of this self-proclaimed "culturally superior empire."

Rome began to splinter. Its citizens had begun to join the early church movement by the thousands, and this corrupt government was not eager to dissolve. Instead of losing dominance, the emperor simply "converted."

In other words, Rome officially adopted Christianity before it was too late. Their domineering ways, on the other hand, did not convert when they nationalized Christianity. Rome kept their militaristic methodology and infused it with Christian orthodoxy. Then as time passed, those in power compiled our Scriptures and twisted them for their own benefit. Even parts of the Gospels became heavily altered to fit a Roman imperial narrative. Especially the Gospel of John, which entirely blamed the Jews, Christ's own people, for the crucifixion.

This devious alteration has been used to spread anti-Semitism for centuries and is still being used by many evangelicals today.

Romans killed Jesus. Not the Jews.

How do we know this?

Many historians concur that both Jewish and Roman law gave the Jewish temple permission to stone heretics as they saw fit. Jesus was labeled a blasphemer in the Bible, and if temple priests, like Caiaphas, wanted to execute Christ, they would have done so legally themselves. Stephen's execution in the book of Acts chapter 7 is an example of their theocratic practice of capital punishment.

When they heard these things, they became enraged and ground their teeth at Stephen. But filled with the Holy Spirit, he gazed into heaven and saw the glory of God and Jesus standing at the right hand of God. "Look," he said, "I see the heavens opened and the Son of Man standing at the right hand of God!" But they covered their ears, and with a loud shout all rushed together against him. Then they dragged him out of the city and began to stone him; and the witnesses laid their coats at the feet of a young man named Saul. While they were stoning Stephen, he prayed, "Lord Jesus, receive my spirit." Then he knelt down and cried out in a loud voice, "Lord, do not hold this sin against them." When he had said this, he died.

Likewise, Jesus would have been stoned by Jewish leaders for blasphemy if heresy had been a claim against Christ. Crucifixion was strictly a Roman practice and priests did not possess the power to command a Roman governor to do their bidding. That's not how military occupation works, and Pilate was not a prefect who casually would take orders from civilians.

The monster known as Pontius Pilate was said to crucify three thousand rebels at a time, and leave their mutilated corpses on display for days as a warning to the Jewish people.

This would haunt Rome when they decided to adopt Christianity.

If you are nationalizing a religion that is centered around a prophet that your government executed, it would behoove you to alter the narrative to portray yourself as innocent. That is exactly what the nationalization of Christianity and the compilation of the Christian canon did.

Rome painted Jewish people as the entities that murdered Christ. Unfortunately, this massive lie is still embraced to this day by many white Christians.

Time moved on, the whitewashing of Jesus continued, and the original message of Jesus would become even more bastardized by colonialism.

If we examine the Christian Doctrine of Discovery, it becomes clear that the church was the driving force behind slavery, genocide, and segregation. This is undeniable, and within our Western churches are relics that prove the racially oppressive history of Christianity.

For example, if Jesus was from Nazareth, then Jesus would have had the physical appearance of someone who is Middle Eastern. In spite of this, portraits of a very white Jesus adorn the walls of many cathedrals around the world.

The cherry on top of the shit cake that is the history of the Church is that the KKK and Nazis both claim to be Christians, and both of them distort the Gospel to spread their manifestos of hate.

Because of this, I believe in many ways white supremacy "killed Jesus."

And … scene!

Didn't see all that coming full circle, did you?

To recap, Jesus was far from white. Christ was a person of color who stood up to the dominant power structure that originated from a group of bloodthirsty white people who thought their way of life was superior to everyone else's.

If the Church wishes to follow Christ's footsteps, then we must reclaim a similar mission. But first, American Christians must come to terms with the racist origins of this faith and this nation without getting defensive.

Many white Christians will argue that they grew up in poverty, and they will use that talking point to deny the existence of white privilege. This is why the "All Lives Matter" movement is so harmful.

Those in power have created a massive distraction by twisting the meaning of "Black Lives Matter." Black Lives Matter was never a humanitarian statement. It is a demand for civil rights. Just because BLACK LIVES SHOULD MATTER, does not mean that ALL LIVES DON'T MATTER. Until the black lives that are lost to unjust imprisonment and police brutality matter in America, then saying "All Lives Matter" is utterly false and will continue to perpetuate the existence of racism in our country.

No one is arguing that poor white people do not experience struggles in life too. We are simply saying that the color of our skin was not a factor in our suffering. It is possible to recognize the inequity caused by colonialism for Natives and people of color while also acknowledging the hurdles that all people face as a result of unbridled capitalism. We have the capacity to acknowledge intersectional dilemmas. Perhaps that is the reason Jesus made room for privileged Gentiles in the revolution against Roman rule.

White Christians must halt our incessant denial of the racist origins of our country and our faith. If we refuse to make amends for our past, then we have forgotten the Rabbi we claim to honor. Without significant reparations to Native peoples and people of color, the faith we claim to uphold is a treacherous imposter. As Christ followers, seeking justice is implied when we claim to uphold the mantra of Jesus.

Owen and I arrived at Jackson's home excited to share the news about our project. In one week's time we had located a hospital bed, acquired new cabinetry, purchased a new toilet, raised funds for new flooring, and acquired donations for plenty of paint.

We sped into the driveway, I ran for the door, and I launched myself up onto the porch. In the process of rushing I accidentally broke a rotting step.

I knocked on the front door, and I began explaining the good news before I even heard a response from the other side.

"Sorry Jackson, I didn't mean to break the porch. I will fix it. In fact, we can fix up the whole place. I got a bunch of donations together, and we can makeover your entire house. We will get everything repaired and looking brand new again," I said excitedly.

But there was no response from inside the home.

I waited a few moments and knocked again.

Still there was nothing.

There was dead silence on the other side of the door.

No static sounds from the TV in the background fuzzing in and out of clarity,

No gravely voice greeting us from within the home,

No soft glow from the lamp on the floor,

There was just deafening silence.

Jackson not being home on a Sunday was quite unusual. I looked back at Owen, and by the look on Owen's face, I was not alone in my concern.

"Maybe Jackson had to go back to the doctor for the infection. We can come back tomorrow," Owen said.

We awoke the next day and made our way back over to Jackson's home. A massive rainstorm had begun by the time we arrived at Jackson's, so I took out my umbrella and slowly made my way through the yard to the door. Dodging mole hills flooding with water, I ascended the stairs far more cautiously than I did the day before.

I knocked once again. Still there was no response.

Discouraged, I walked back to the car.

"Perhaps Jackson had to be admitted to the hospital for an extended stay?" I thought nervously.

We went home concerned for our friend, and decided to return later in the week.

Two days later I pulled into the driveway to find several people on the property painting and repairing the house. It appeared that someone had the same idea we did.

A burly, middle-aged contractor wearing a flannel shirt approached my car and was obviously curious about the nature of my visit.

"Looks like y'all beat us to it. We would be happy to help y'all remodel. We will do anything to help Jackson out," I said firmly, shaking the contractor's hand.

"Y'all didn't hear? I am really sorry to be the one that has to tell y'all this, but Jackson died last week," said the contractor solemnly.

I stood there in shock.

"Why did you wait so long to do something, Christopher, you idiot?" I thought.

I made my way back down to my waterfront sanctuary to reflect. I watched shrimp boats come and go for hours as I sat pondering this difficult news.

How many opportunities for good are before us on a daily basis that go unnoticed? How often had my privilege blinded me to the suffering of the marginalized, when I possessed the capacity to do something about their suffering?

In this time of inner dialogue, I realized that our noble ambitions to help Jackson were merely a Band-Aid on a festering wound. We simply did not need to improve Jackson's house. We need to be actively rewriting policy that causes Jackson's level of poverty to exist in the first place. Our intent was pure, but our efforts ultimately would have made a small ripple in the ocean that is white supremacy.

The reality is that the hard work of anti-racism is far from over, and our work has to be bigger than just showing up to provide relief from oppression when it suits our sense of fulfillment. We must fight to end the root cause of these conditions entirely.

Our work is bigger than patching up dilapidated shacks. The restorative work of the historical Jesus beckons Christ followers to the front lines of resistance and demands that systemic racism be yanked from America's soil root and stem.

A just future is possible, but not until the Church can confess the sins of our ancestors that fashioned the foundation of the many injustices that surround us. Dr. King said it best in these famous words,

"The time is always right, to do what is right."

CENTURIONS

I immediately threw my rainbow-colored protest sign that read ...

"Divorced Christians Don't Get to Judge Anyone's Marriage.
-Sincerely, Pissed Off Clergy"

... and fell to the ground. I barely avoided the scalding hot waffle fries being hurled at my face. My evasive maneuver was clearly an overreaction, but I did not have time to process the exact nature of the projectile that was launched in my direction. As a southern person of mostly Irish descent, and lover of all-things-fried, fresh crispy potatoes are among my preferred items with which to be assaulted.

I dusted myself off and furiously glared at my spud-flinging adversary who was driving a green Toyota Sequoia just outside of the Chick-fil-A drive-thru. Without hesitation, I proceeded to unleash a series of wholesome four-letter spiritual adjectives in order to ascertain the reason for this conflict.

"WHAT THE FUCK?' I yelled at my attacker, who had the appearance of someone named Karen, Cathy, Becky, or Debra.

(Caucasian, bob hairstyle, massive sunglasses, blond highlights, Salt Life sticker on the rear window, bedazzled jeans, smokes Virginia Slims, mid-40s, speaks to management a lot. You know the type.)

"Some pastor you are, cursing like that," said my newly acquainted, upper-middle-class nemesis while taunting me with their bag of fresh fast food.

It never ceases to amaze me that confronting evangelical or conservative bullshit somehow invites their aggression. They get so critical when you defend yourself. Even when their harmful behavior, like throwing scalding hot food at someone, is the greater offense. God forbid a Christian curse in frustration because someone assaulted them.

"There is freedom of religion in the USA. Love it or leave it," Debra said just before speeding off. (The more I think about it, "Debra" just feels like the right name.)

As the SUV turned the corner, I was less than surprised to see Jesus fish (plural) scattered about the tailgate adjacent to American flag bumper stickers loaded with anti-liberal propaganda.

It would have been nice to have had some backup in this altercation, but I was the only pastor protesting the Chick-fil-A Appreciation Day created by Mike Huckabee. To be honest, in this mostly Republican city, I was the only one protesting period.

The year was 2012 and many progressives had just become aware that Dan Cathy and Chick-fil-A were supporting organizations with anti-LGBTQ initiatives in America, and anti-LGBTQ Christian extremist groups in Africa. Organizations like Focus on the Family Institute, the American Family Association, the National Organization for Marriage, the Pennsylvania Family Institute, Exodus International, and the Family Research Council were being sponsored with the company's profits and with Cathy's personal finances. So progressives took to the internet to object to this unethical use of corporate and executive finances.

Mike Huckabee countered this protest with a rallying call for people to support Dan Cathy's company on their breakfast/lunch/dinner breaks on this day that, according to them, was a "celebration of religious freedom."

In my mind, this was a needed opportunity to make a statement concerning the hypocrisy of evangelical anti-LGBTQ theology.

I hoped that I would arrive at the local franchise of Chick-fil-A to witness a crowd of protesters marching with their signs and chanting into their bullhorns, but apparently that was wishful thinking in the Low Country.

Throughout the day, I was cursed, called derogatory names, and threatened with physical violence. Mostly by people with the nerve to claim that they worshipped the same God that I do.

It was evident that day that historical Jesus and evangelical Jesus couldn't possibly be the same person, nor could they be more opposed to one another.

———— |———

My next topic of discourse is so much bigger than sexual identity. It is about the various relationships, liberties, and sexual encounters that the Church restricts based on a poor understanding of scripture. There is a massive difference between what Christians presume the Bible says about sex and marriage, and what the Bible ACTUALLY says about sex and marriage.

The Bible is in fact filled with directives that endorse specific sexual ethics, but unfortunately none of these guidelines are consistent throughout the collective narrative of scripture.

Let's begin this section by defining what most modern-day conservative Christians assume that the Bible commands regarding sexual ethics and our individual marital dynamics. Evangelical fundamentalists believe that the Bible condemns any sexual activity outside the confines of heterosexual matrimony. Within these perceived limitations of marriage and intercourse, many evangelicals believe that every wife should fully submit to her husband's will. Finally, within the Christian fundamentalist demographic there is a significant portion of people who identify as pro-life, and some of them refuse to accept any method of birth control.

These restrictions of relational, sexual, and reproductive conduct are among the most definitive qualities associated with American Christianity. Regrettably, for a substantial portion of my life I aligned my belief system with every trait listed in the paragraph above. Many adherents to the Christian faith are manipulated by an agenda that leads them to similar conclusions, but these beliefs about marriage, sex, sexuality, gender roles, and gender identity are not based in any amount of contextual biblical evidence.

That is why this conversation matters.

In order to discuss these topics effectively, we must examine each conservative assumption regarding sexuality, gender roles, intercourse, and marriage individually.

EVANGELICAL ASSUMPTION #1: MARRIAGE SHOULD BE MONOGAMOUS

Before we begin, I am remarried and I will say that my spouse and I are happily monogamous by choice and we feel that, for our relationship, it is a good choice. However, our decision to be monogamous is a personal decision that is not based in our spiritual beliefs, because the vast majority of scripture does not promote healthy marital dynamics. In truth, a contextual "biblical marriage" is a practice that should never be resurrected.

The Bible promotes polygamy and what some call patriarchal polyamory. Patriarchal polyamory was a sexual privilege that allowed multiple sexual partners, but it was exclusively a privilege for husbands only.

In fact, there is an entire book of the Old Testament that is dedicated to the sexual escapades of a polygamous patriarch by the name of Solomon.

Songs of Solomon may be one of the most misunderstood books in the Bible. Evangelicals constantly attempt to make Songs of Solomon more wholesome than it was intended to be. This book is so charged with sexual energy that Jewish children were not allowed to read it until they became adults. Many preachers try to repackage this biblical entry as a graphic depiction of a monogamous couple and their impassioned romance, but this kind of censored interpretation is diluting the provocative nature of Songs of Solomon to fit within the parameters of fundamentalist purity culture.

Not only is Songs of Solomon a collection of erotic encounters, it isn't even a love story between two people. It is basically a journal of one person's documented sexual milestones with wives, concubines, and mistresses.

Solomon had seven hundred wives and three hundred concubines according to Songs of Solomon chapter six.

I often wonder why this *50 Shades of Yahweh* is even in the Bible

One of my favorite ministerial memories of Songs of Solomon is from my days with a collegiate Bible study. We had been meeting as a home group for months. It was an extremely intimate gathering that was far more focused on quality fellowship than spending time in exegesis. As young adults working multiple jobs, we were more than fine with this low-key model of Christian community.

Our pastor, on the other hand, was not fine with it. Our church leadership insisted that we come up with a logo and select an official Bible verse that would capture the essence of our study's vision and values. We initially objected to this directive, but I was commanded to submit to pastoral council and follow the instruction of our anointed leader ... and there was something else they wanted the group to do, but I wasn't listening.

None of us were eager to submit to the whims of a dictator, and our group was kind of a band of pseudo-troublemakers anyway. Take away drugs, sex, tobacco, and alcohol from young adults and pranks will be the lifeblood that they will crave. I guarantee it.

So for our verse we picked Songs of Solomon 7:7-8, which reads,

Your stature is like a palm tree, And your breasts are like its fruit.

I say to you, "I will climb this palm tree, And take hold of its fruit."

For our logo we had a clip art stick figure standing on top of a ladder that was leaning on a palm tree. The stick figure on top of the ladder was depicted with outstretched hands that reached toward two large coconuts hanging in the palm tree.

Below our graphic masterpiece were the words "Songs of Solomon 7:7-8," but we did not include the actual scripture. We had this logo printed on T-shirts, patches, and stickers, and we flew this inside joke under the wire for almost two years without getting caught.

My point is that this extremely sensual book of the Bible is so rarely ever read that people do not know what it says, and many are truly shocked when they discover the polyamorous nature of Songs of Solomon.

Solomon was not the only polygamous/polyamorous character in the Hebrew Bible. There were plenty of prominent Old Testament characters with multiple lovers. Abraham, Esau, Ezra, Caleb, Gideon, David, Jacob, Saul, and Hosea are all examples of Old Testament polygamists with multiple spouses and/or concubines.

So where does the concept of "biblical marriage" being monogamous come from?

Two places.

The first of which is found "in the beginning" of the Bible.

See what I did there?

Literalists understand Adam and Eve as historical figures, and assume that God literally made these two people to enjoy paradise together. For them, Adam and Eve are the standard for the modern institution of marriage. We already have discussed how reading the first eleven chapters of Genesis as a literal document is bad theology, but by the time we get to the twelfth chapter of Genesis we can start taking the characters of Genesis a little more literally.

The key phrase here is "a little."

Chapter twelve of Genesis discusses the origins of the twelve tribes of Israel. This anthology of the twelve tribes of Israel began with a polygamist named Abraham, and according to the Bible Abraham also had sex with concubines. Abraham, one of the most significant figures in the Old Testament, was a polygamist.

Interestingly, as we continue to read through the Old Testament, the practice of polygamy is never condemned, and we do not see monogamy appear until the New Testament.

So why is there an obvious disconnect in the Scriptures?

The earliest followers of Jesus were Jewish, and many scholars who are both secular and progressive Christians believe that Jews in the early church would have seen no issue with polygamy.

NONE.

As I have pointed out multiple times in this book, the official religion of "Christianity" would be birthed as a Roman belief system almost two centuries after Christ died. Not only was the hellenistic concept of Heaven and Hell inserted into the New Testament after Rome adopted Christianity, but Rome injected their value of monogamous marriage into the text as well. This is why there is a clear contradiction in regards to marital practices between the two testaments of the Bible.

In short, the Bible does not promote a consistent theme or design in regards to matrimony.

EVANGELICAL ASSUMPTION #2: WIVES SHOULD SUBMIT TO THEIR HUSBANDS

The Bible describes ancient societies that were highly patriarchal. The Jewish people of the Bible did not just treat women as if they were socially inferior. The primitive peoples of this day considered women to be property and often viewed women as breeding stock. In the story of Abraham and Sarah that is found in Genesis, Sarah refers to Abraham as "lord," and that language is indicative of the kind of sexist society that they lived in. In many cases, women in this time and culture functioned as glorified slaves.

Today the modernized version of this harmful ideology no longer considers brides to be a product to be sold and purchased. This is an improvement, but more progress for feminism is needed in our spiritual communities. Many churches still demand the submission of women to men. This vile culture of abuse goes far beyond husbands forcing their wives to submit. These communities do not approve anyone who identifies as a woman to be a leader in any capacity, and these churches openly refuse the possibility of ordaining women as clergy. This anti-woman culture is a byproduct of blending ancient misogyny with modern theology, and it was an active contributor in cultivating our current patriarchy.

It is an undeniable fact that the Bible was crafted by chauvinistic cultures. Though many egalitarians would disagree with me, I believe that pretending that the Scriptures were written with a modern message of gender equality dishonors the noble heroism of women in the Bible that existed in a male dominant society and overcame massive patriarchal obstacles in their rise to greatness.

Characters like:

Miriam, a prophet who was an ancient worship leader and composer of a captivating song in Exodus.

Or Deborah, a mighty judge and war general who presided over the people of Israel.

Or Jael, an assassin who was essential in defeating the Canaanites.

Or Mary Magdalene, an apostle of Jesus who solely was responsible for financing the early church in its formative years. Mary was also the first person to declare that Christ had risen.

That is right, y'all. Mary Magdalene was the O. G. evangelist!

There are multiple prophets, deacons, and heroes who identify as women in the Scriptures. If we are to truly recognize and value their legacy, then we cannot ignore the sexist climate that they overcame on their path to authority.

EVANGELICAL ASSUMPTION #3: PREMARITAL SEX IS FORBIDDEN

This belief system is vital for the purity movement, and it is the reason that abstinence initiatives still exist. Virginity in the evangelical mind is a sacred thing that should not be tainted before matrimony. When evangelicals promote their concept of biblical sexual purity, they need to understand that even their "conservative views" of biblical virginity are sugarcoating a horrifically toxic ancient belief system. Little do they know that their standard of self-induced sexual deprivation was unjustly applied to women alone in biblical times.

In biblical times, a woman's sexuality literally belonged to their father before they were married. Not because their father wanted to protect their daughter's honor, but because their father wanted to protect an investment. Fathers would sell/trade their daughters to a suitor that they deemed acceptable. If someone wanted to marry a young maiden, the maiden's father would be offered a trade agreement for the young maiden's hand in marriage. Virgins were sought after by bachelors, thus they were more expensive.

In those times, if someone were to rape a woman before marriage, then that woman was required to marry the rapist according to the book of Leviticus. Although marrying a rapist was dependent on the father of the bride being fairly compensated for the bride. If the father did not approve of this union, or if the rapist did not want to commit to marriage, then the rapist was still required to pay the father for a financial loss. This is because a woman who was not a virgin had little financial value within the culture of this time. Thus, the rapist had to repay the father for the lost economic value of the daughter.

For the people of ancient Israel, marriage was a business; women were the supply, and virgins were the greatest demand.

However, bachelors were not required to be virgins before marriage at all.

This double standard of biblical purity culture is even more evident when we read that there was virtually no punishment in Levitical law for men if they committed sexual assault.

It is 2019 and not a fucking thing has changed!

I think part of the reason the Church has such an emphasis on virginity is our collective misunderstanding of Mary and Joseph's relationship. First and foremost, Mary just like any other Jewish maiden of that time, was being sold to Joseph. Mary was around thirteen years of age when this transaction occurred, and many scholars believe that Joseph was likely somewhere between forty and fifty years of age.

This means that the person who brought Christ into our world was a child bride forced to engage in a pedophiliac relationship. For me, this is further proof that these ancient customs should have no place in modern relationships.

Perhaps the greatest misunderstanding about the Nativity story is Mary's chastity. Mary was not a virgin. The word for "virgin" in the Nativity comes from a Greek mistranslation of a Hebrew prophecy in the book of Isaiah that says,

> *Therefore the Lord himself will give you a sign. Look, the young maiden is with child and shall bear a son, and shall name him Immanuel.*

The word for "young maiden" in Isaiah is the Hebrew word *almah*. In the Nativity story found in the the the Gospel of Matthew, this prophecy was reiterated to drive home the claim of Christ being the Messiah. The Koine Greek word *parthenos* was erroneously inserted when it was translated from Isaiah.

The word *parthenos* literally means "virgin," but we know that this translation in the Gospel of Matthew was an error, because the ancient Hebrew dialect had a word for virgin, *bethulah,* and it is used throughout the Old Testament to describe virginity. The author of Matthew transcribed this Old Testament prophecy incorrectly, and it was likely on purpose.

Divine impregnation of a virgin was an essential mythological ingredient in origin stories of Roman and Greek demigods. Perseus, Mythra, Romulus, Remus, and many other characters were all born of virgins. When Rome nationalized Christianity as its official religion, the virgin birth of Christ made this institutional transition more palatable to Gentiles. We talked about this practice of cultural appropriation to get public approval in the chapter titled "Idols."

Nowhere in the original language of scripture does it say that Mary was a virgin. It simply says that Mary was young. This implies that Mary had a sexual encounter before being "promised" to Joseph (aka sold to Joseph).

Perhaps Mary's pregnancy was the result of a moment of passion with a secret lover. Maybe this impregnation was due to Mary being sexually assaulted. Either way, the moment Mary conceived, this toxic male-dominant society considered Mary to be worth less in a financial transaction and worthless within their misogynistic system of class.

Yet the Nativity of Luke assigns monumental value to Mary.

By no longer being a virgin, Mary lost favor in the eyes of society, but according to Gabriel, Mary found favor above all others in the eyes of God.

The message of the Nativity is one that we see today time and time again in Christendom. The Church tells young adults that their most precious mission in life is in denying themselves and their sexual cravings. If they stumble, they are somehow tainted and have lost value in God's eyes.

That is bullshit!

The Gospel declares that God finds favor in us all regardless of whether or not we choose to respectfully engage in sexual intimacy. This is why I believe that when it comes to sexual encounters between consenting adults, it is time for the Church to shut the bedroom door.

The Bible has far more to say about people sleeping on the streets, than what grown-ass folks consent to do under their sheets.

EVANGELICAL ASSUMPTION #4: ABORTION IS A SIN

It pains me that after hundreds of years not much has changed in regard to toxic masculinity. Straight evangelical men still fight tooth and nail for legislation that regulates what women can do with their own bodies by manipulating women around them with the Bible to oppose a woman's right to choose.

This baffles me for two reasons.

First off, the Bible doesn't oppose abortions directly.

Ancient Hebrews believed that life begins and ends with breath. They believed that spirit and breath were one in the same. You can Google the Hebrew term for breath (*ruah)* and the Koine Greek word for breath (*pnuema)* if you'd like for more information on this fascinating topic.

Secondly, the Bible clearly endorses conditional abortion in the fifth chapter of Numbers.

The book of Numbers says,

> *The priest is then to take a handful of the grain offering as a memorial offering and burn it on the altar; after that, he is to have the woman drink the water. If she has made herself impure and been unfaithful to her husband, this will be the result: When she is made to drink the water that brings a curse and causes bitter suffering, it will enter her, her abdomen will swell and her womb will miscarry, and she will become a curse.*

That's right. This is the only verse in the entirety of scripture that discusses any process resembling an abortion. The Bible permitted ritualistic abortions as long as a suspicious husband felt that there might have be an instance of infidelity that caused their spouse's pregnancy. This verse is just one of many that illuminates the influence that toxic masculinity had on this ancient society.

EVANGELICAL ASSUMPTION #5: LGBTQ+ FOLKS ARE SINNING

1 Corinthians chapter six says this:

> *Do you not know that wrongdoers will not inherit the kingdom of God? Do not be deceived! Fornicators, idolaters, adulterers, homosexuals, thieves, the greedy, drunkards, revilers, robbers—none of these will inherit the kingdom of God. And this is what some of*

you used to be. But you were washed, you were sanctified, you were justified in the name of the Lord Jesus Christ and in the Spirit of our God.

This verse has a lot to say about the culture of Rome, but it says nothing contextually about differing sexual identities. The word wrongly translated as "homosexual" in English comes from the Koine Greek word *arsenokoitais*. It is a very tricky word to translate, because Paul seems to be one of the few people to have used it historically. It rarely is found in ancient Greek writings. This is odd, because the Koine Greek language had many words for "homosexual." The most common was *pathikos*.

Strangely, *pathikos* is not found anywhere in the entire composition of the New Testament.

So what was Paul talking about?

Arsenokoitais was actually a word in other ancient texts referencing a Roman citizen who took advantage of the Roman temple tax. Many Romans at this time used prostitutes in worship rituals. If you were a good Roman citizen, and paid your taxes on time, then you had access to temple "prostitutes." These were not willing sex workers like many people in the industry today. The Roman temple system actually used slaves for their prostitutes to encourage people to pay their taxes. The worst part about this was that many of these slaves were very small children.

In proper context this verse is not condemning "homosexuality," but rather it is condemning pedophilia. This verse in 1 Corinthians was shaming people who took advantage of legalized sex trafficking and those that sexually abused kids. This is why Christians should stop oppressing others by fighting to end marriage equality and get their asses to the front lines to combat child brides and sex trafficking. Those are sins that The Bible actually addressed!

Also, did you know that the term "homosexual" did not even appear in English translations of the Bible until 1946? The original phrase translated into English for *arsenokoitais* was "sexually immoral."

You can Google it if you'd like. My book will wait.

This false translation stemmed from bigoted political agendas and has caused massive amounts of misinformation, heartache, and abuse in the Church.

Every word in the Bible that is translated to English as "homosexual" or "sexual immorality" means "rapist," "pedophile," or "greedy" in context.

There is no room for Christians to "agree to disagree" about this anymore.

The Church has become a place that is unsafe and unwelcoming for LGBTQ citizens and, ironically, a haven for rapists and pedophiles.

The time for coddling bigots in the Church is over. God's children aren't safe if intolerance is tolerated. LGBTQ folks should not need sanctuary while they are in our sanctuaries!

I usually find that I need more than the information above in debates concerning the topic of sexual identity with conservatives. The following story is a silver bullet in most of those arguments.

There is a passage of scripture in the Gospel of Matthew that many conservatives are familiar with. This verse has a hidden meaning that completely refutes all non-LGBTQ affirming interpretations of Christian doctrine.

This message of affirmation for LGBTQ folks to which I am referring is not found in anything that Christ said, but rather what Christ did NOT say when given the opportunity to discuss sexuality.

The story begins in the eighth chapter of Matthew:

> *When he entered Capernaum, a centurion came to him, appealing to him and saying, "Lord, my servant is lying at home paralyzed, in terrible distress." And he said to him, "I will come and cure him." The centurion answered, "Lord, I am not worthy to have you come under my roof; but only speak the word, and my servant will be healed. For I also am a man under authority, with soldiers under me; and I say to one, 'Go,' and he goes, and to another, 'Come,' and he comes, and to my slave, 'Do this,' and the slave does it." When Jesus heard him, he was amazed and said to those who followed him, "Truly I tell you, in no one in Israel have I found such faith."*

Remember during the time of Christ there were palpable tensions between Rome and the Jewish community. Because of this, the fact that the centurion approaches Jesus in this passage implies that this Gentile's request for healing from a rabbi likely is a last resort.

Now let's unpack the rest of this story.

The word "servant" in this passage comes from the Koine Greek word *pais,* and it does not mean "servant." *Pais* literally means "male lover," although many conservative concordances will say otherwise.

The existence of a *pais* in scripture should not surprise anyone who has a basic understanding of ancient Roman culture. Rome was very accepting of differing sexual orientations. Especially when compared to Western cultures today. Christ was immersed in a value system where sexuality was vastly accepted as fluid.

Despite being surrounded by various sexual identities, Jesus totally was uninterested in mentioning sexuality in the Gospels. Even when given the opportunity to condemn the centurion and the *pais* in this story, Jesus is silent. Christ healed the dying *pais* and said absolutely nothing about this couple's sexuality. Christ's silence in this story should scream volumes to the Church. If we believe Christ is the lens through which we interpret the text, then where Jesus was quiet we should be too, and that logic should be applied from every pulpit around the globe.

Yet, the evangelical church has been almost solely responsible for LGBTQ suicides and homelessness in America. Many teenagers are sleeping on the streets because their parents abandoned them due to the ungodly amount of venomous misinformation being regurgitated by the Church. This especially is true for the trans community.

The book of Galatians says:

> *There is no longer Jew or Greek, there is no longer slave or free, there is no longer man and woman; for all of you are one in Christ Jesus.*

Here is biblical evidence for breaking the binary, and evangelical people who claim to uphold scripture as their ultimate authority on all things are the biggest inhibition for allowing progress in this area that could literally save the lives of countless Americans.

If gender identity doesn't matter "in Christ," then why the fuck does it matter in our churches?

To bring all of this together: I do not believe that Jesus gave two shits about condemning humanity's sexual orientations, marital dynamics, gender identities, or consensual encounters. Christ cared about ending injustices and breaking societal chains. Christ had no intent to impose the concept of abstinence or to retrain our erotic appetites.

I believe that if adults engage in sex that is respectful, mutually agreed upon, and that honors the bodily temple that God gave us, then we can do so as we deem fit as long as we take our afterglow back to the frontline of the resistance.

———◄ ►———

That Sunday, I made some homemade chicken chili, hot water cornbread, blackberry basil lemonade, and macaroni and cheese for our worship service. I loaded the food, our portable sound gear, our communion set, and our sports equipment into my Prius and headed to the park for worship.

Ten minutes before our service began, we saw that no one was present for church other than our core team. I was puzzled by our scarce attendance and so was my team. For months, we consistently had a weekly attendance of at least fifty to seventy people.

It was a brutally hot day, so we concluded that the poor weather conditions must have been the culprit.

That is when our parishioner, Sebastian, approached our tables. Sebastian was around forty years old and never failed to show up for a game of basketball. Sebastian was always a cheerful soul. Today would be different. Today our friend was quite noticeably a bearer of bad news.

With a sigh Sebastian looked at the ground, chuckled lightly, and said, "Y'all didn't think they were coming, did you?"

"Of course we did," I laughed, assuming that the question was a joke.

Sebastian looked around and realized that we were all entirely oblivious as to why our attendance had dropped.

"You all have no idea, do you?" asked Sebastian.

"What is with all the rhetorical questions? Of course we don't know what is going on. What happened, Sebastian?" I asked.

"A lot of local churches mentioned the Chick-fil-A protest in several sermons this morning. They named you specifically, Christopher, and warned their congregations about your heretical beliefs, and talk moves fast in this town, y'all.

"Like it or not, you all have been officially labeled a cult by every church in the county. No one is coming today, and they certainly aren't going to let their children attend a 'pro-gay' church.

"Their words by the way, not mine," Sebastian added, compassionately trying to ease the blow of this news.

Still, we were all totally stunned.

Did those relationships mean nothing? Did months of our time and resources go up in smoke because of one political action?

We immediately got on our cell phones and called our congregants to see where they were. Our calls either went straight to voicemail, or we were asked to never call again.

Despite the work we had done, regardless of the connections we had made, we had been officially shunned.

If there was ever divine confirmation that my dream for a progressive church in the Low Country was impossible, it was this.

I was arrogant enough to believe that I possessed the capacity to influence southern conservative Christianity. I am not saying that the South is incapable of changing, but I realized that day that I was certainly not qualified to lead a reformation of the Bible Belt at this point in my life.

For weeks I was devastated, but my best friend Sean called me that night, and once again spoke wisdom into my life.

Sean advised me to search for a church planting position in a politically blue state. The next day I began exploring the possibility of leaving the South and moving west. I reached out to my friend and colleague who was the director of a church planting network and inquired about possible places to start a new church within the Disciples of Christ.

Weeks later, I was presented with several openings around the United States to plant a new church in my denomination.

I spent the rest of the year selling my possessions so I could afford to relocate, and I prepared to say goodbye to this so-called "Bible Belt." I have always thought that this was an odd name for the South.

If the Deep South is the "Bible Belt," then it is no wonder that America's pants are around its ankles.

Still, it was the only home I had ever known.

I will forever have fond memories of southern cuisine, exquisite craft beers, amazing music, and the wonderful souls with whom I collided during the formative and transformative years of my career.

The sounds of a tin roof being assaulted by weekly thunderstorms, the excitement of SEC football season beginning in autumn, and the smell of the damp pluff mud creeping into your nostrils when approaching coastal marsh lands are sensations that can never truly leave someone.

Those recollections will never fade. Neither will the scars and heartbreak that I acquired during my tenure in the motherland of American conservative fundamentalism.

TRANSFIGURATION

The sky danced with a fiery glow as the sun descended over the Pacific waters before me. Purple, red, and golden beams showered the horizon. Pelicans soared effortlessly overhead, and the echo of barking sea lions could be heard in the distance as they chanted their challenges for dominance. Otters emerged briefly and playfully. They twirled in excitement while clasping their treasured morsels of mollusks and shellfish as they lounged on their backs in their aquatic utopia.

As I watched this glorious sunset retreat behind a nautical veil, I sat in awe of this tapestry of creation being sketched by nature's abundance. I sat in wonder as I waited anxiously for a needed sign.

Years of debating whether I should stay in the Bible Belt or journey west was still an unsettled trajectory in my heart.

Beyond the breathtaking artistry of the Santa Cruz sunset before me loomed a decision that I had put off for months. Like the light that slowly vanished from our closest star and that was fading softly into the sea, so was my ability to procrastinate a final decision any longer.

The months following the Chick-fil-A protest were consumed with searching for possible opportunities of employment outside of the Bible Belt. For various reasons, the marshlands that had once provided a sense of security now felt like a trap that I could not escape. This was discouraging for many reasons, but luckily I had found two possibilities for a new beginning.

I could choose to stay on the East Coast and take a worship leader position with excellent benefits and substantial pay at a new progressive church in Washington, D.C.; or I could take an opportunity to plant a new church in Santa Cruz, California, with a free facility promised to our new church once their pastor retired.

I had to experience both cities before I could decide which opportunity I would choose.

The pastor of the Santa Cruz church flew me out for three days to examine the city. To be honest, I wasn't initially convinced that California would be a good fit for me. Before I had arrived in Santa Cruz, I assumed that I would be moving to Virginia. The job in D.C. was part-time, and the pay was more than I had ever been offered for full-time positions.

I had visited Southern California in my past, and it was not a place that I could personally call home. Years before this moment I had been to Los Angeles, and I toured the city when my flight was delayed. It is a wonderful place, but L.A. is too fast-paced for my preference. I also had visited Bakersfield, California, and if you have ever been to Bakersfield, then you would understand my apprehension about California.

However, I began to slowly lose interest in the worship leader job in Washington, D.C., the moment I arrived in California. This unique place on the Pacific Coast was paradise, and its magnificence was drawing me in.

The scenery surrounding Santa Cruz is breathtaking. There are mountainous trails shaded by glorious redwood trunks towering far overhead concealing the sun. The beaches teem with marine life and natural bridge formations near the coastal cliffs. Parks nestle closely to state forests that serve as sanctuaries for migrating monarch butterflies. Massive great white sharks and elephant seals often gather along the edge of the coast.

The cherry on top of this delicious destination is that my favorite animals, humpback whales, are known to leap from the sea as they feed on schools of fish that gather by the pier. I had hoped to witness such a miracle, but was left in wanting when I explored the boardwalk earlier that day.

Santa Cruz was nothing like Southern California. It is laid-back and incredibly progressive both socially and politically. Santa Cruz is one of the most liberal cities in the United States, with an incredibly young population and a strong activist demographic. Yet, Santa Cruz did not have any progressive churches with a millennial audience within the city limits.

This place seemed to be a perfect fit for my ministry, but I was still unsure of where I should go.

The temperature dropped in tandem with the daylight. There was a glowing bar resting on top of the water where the sun had rested just moments prior. The breeze raced across the deep waters to the cliff on which I sat. A chill stung my skin, and I knew I would have to make my way back to my room soon, where I fully expected to be up all night deliberating where I belonged.

I took one last glimpse of the masterpiece before me, and I will never forget what happened next.

A few hundred feet from the edge of the cliff the waters began to churn. Gulls in the distance frantically rushed to the newly forming whirlpool. Within seconds small fish lunged aggressively from within the aquatic disruption. Then right through the middle of the chaotic school of sardines, burst a humpback whale in full breach. This titan lunged effortlessly from the depths and its skin glowed with the reflection of twilight as its massive body crashed back into the waves. Not once, not twice, but three times this barnacled ballerina danced before my eyes. As if I needed more sugar with this medicine, its calf attempted to mimic this behavior over and over again. A fierce sense of wonder and gratitude overcame my soul.

Time had frozen. I stood paralyzed, breath stilled, jaw unhinged, chills up my spine, and tears pooling in the corner of my eyes.

I didn't have to debate where I belonged anymore. The most majestic of God's creatures announced that I was home.

Perhaps I was a fool for taking career advice in this chance encounter with an oceanic behemoth, but isn't that exactly what biblical faith is? Finding supernatural meaning within our natural world.

Voices from burning bushes,

Rainbows declaring peace,

Invitations in baked grains,

and remembering a new promise in a cup.

———————

I tend to get so wrapped up in the material world since I have adopted progressive Christianity, that I often neglect holy moments that are always around me. There are so many components of the material world that are truly sacred, and the Bible has a lot to say about our existence being a miracle.

The book of Exodus reads:

> The Lord said to Moses, "I will do the very thing that you have asked; for you have found favor in my sight, and I know you by name." Moses said, "Show me your glory, I pray." And he said,

"I will make all my goodness pass before you, and will proclaim before you the name, 'The Lord'; and I will be gracious to whom I will be gracious, and will show mercy on whom I will show mercy. But," he said, "you cannot see my face; for no one shall see me and live." And the Lord continued, "See, there is a place by me where you shall stand on the rock; and while my glory passes by I will put you in a cleft of the rock, and I will cover you with my hand until I have passed by; then I will take away my hand, and you shall see my back; but my face shall not be seen." Be ready in the morning, and come up in the morning to Mount Sinai and present yourself there to me, on the top of the mountain. No one shall come up with you, and do not let anyone be seen throughout all the mountain; and do not let flocks or herds graze in front of that mountain."

The term "God's back" doesn't mean a physical back. For ancient Jewish people, their God was spirit and breath. Which is why the name *YHWH,* or Yahweh, is so significant in the Old Testament. This name is meant to mimic a breathing sound. Their God did not have a bodily form according to ancient Judaic beliefs.

But why does God have a "back" in this story?

The Hebrew term for "God's back" is *ahar.* There is no one word in common vernacular that captures the essence of what *ahar* means. Although some theologians assert that it simply means "after." However, that definition does not capture the essence of the message within this fantastical encounter.

Ahar basically means where the entirety of someone's presence had formerly been. Like when you think that you are having a conversation with someone who was just behind you.

Later in this passage, Moses was commanded to chisel two large tablets of stone and bring them up the mountain. These tablets would be used for the inscription of the Ten Commandments.

Notice how God said, *"Come up to the mountain and present yourself on top of the mountain."* Is there a reason for this redundancy?

So if you were hiking a mountain trail while carrying two heavy stone tablets all the way to the summit, what is the first thing you think about when you finally reach the top?

If you are me, you would think, "Shit! How the hell am I going to get down?"

I think that is what most people would do in this situation as well.

I think God wanted Moses' complete attention, which is why God said there were to be no animals grazing, or people occupying the valley below the mountain when Moses reached the summit. In this story I think God was saying, *"Go to the top of the mountain and be present mentally at the top of the mountain. Don't let anything obstruct your view Moses. Don't get distracted."*

The text continues:

> So Moses cut two tablets of stone like the former ones; and he rose early in the morning and went up on Mount Sinai, as the Lord had commanded him, and took in his hand the two tablets of stone. The Lord descended in the cloud and stood with him there, and proclaimed the name, "The Lord." The Lord passed before him, and proclaimed, "the Lord, a God merciful and gracious, slow to anger, and abounding in steadfast love and faithfulness, keeping steadfast love for the thousandth generation, forgiving iniquity and transgression and sin, yet by no means clearing the guilty, but

visiting the iniquity of the parents upon the children, and the children's children, to the third and the fourth generation."

And Moses quickly bowed his head toward the earth, and worshiped. He said, "If now I have found favor in your sight, O Lord, I pray, let the Lord go with us. Although this is a stiff-necked people, pardon our iniquity and our sin, and take us for your inheritance."

So Moses listened to God pass by while Moses' eyes were concealed and God basically told Moses,

"I am the God of love. I am the God of mercy. I am the God of justice. I am God."

Then after hearing God's qualities, Moses regained sight.

What is the first thing that Moses saw?

God's back.

What is God's back?

Where God's presence had just been.

Where is Moses located when this happens?

On top of a mountain. Looking down at the valley.

Moses was viewing all of creation in its glorious entirety after being in the presence of God. Then, according to Exodus, Moses descended from the mountain with a face that glowed from being in God's presence.

What does this mean? It means so many things!

First, it means that this God cannot be contained within the parameters of a physical body. God is everywhere and dwells within all that is good on this earth. It means that God is not just a force of love, mercy, and justice. God IS love, mercy, and justice.

They should really rename that section of Exodus, "Moses gets woke."

This is why the commandment that God gave Moses that says "You shall have no graven images" is significant. Because once you make a depiction of a God, you can understand that deity. In essence, you can insert limitations into that being, and a restricted entity is not the god that ancient Hebrews or the early church worshiped. Their god was much more of a force that was totally unbound by mortal parameters.

The Judaic faith worshipped a god they knew that they could never fully grasp. Doubt was pivotal to their faith. That is why I think it is heresy to view the Bible as the ultimate source of truth. Ancient Jewish people welcomed questioning, and they believed that the knowledge of the universe would be revealed to humanity slowly throughout time. These ancient sages believed that no matter how much we learn, humanity can never fully comprehend the entirety of existence.

Even though Moses' story in Exodus is technically primitive wisdom, there is not a scientist alive who would argue against the belief that humanity will maintain an eternally limited capacity to grasp the vastness of the cosmos, space, and time. Our pursuit of discovery will surely be an immortal endeavor.

Another biblical story that strikes a similar chord to this passage in Exodus comes from the ninth chapter of the Gospel of Mark.

Six days later, Jesus took with him Peter and James and John, and led them up a high mountain apart, by themselves. And he was transfigured before them, and his clothes became dazzling white, such as no one on earth could bleach them. And there appeared to them Elijah with Moses, who were talking with Jesus. Then Peter said to Jesus, "Rabbi, it is good for us to be here; let us make three dwellings, one for you, one for Moses, and one for Elijah." He did not know what to say, for they were terrified. Then a cloud overshadowed them, and from the cloud there came a voice, "This is my Son, the Beloved; listen to him!" Suddenly when they looked around, they saw no one with them any more, but only Jesus.

Did you see the similarities in these two stories? Let's dig a little deeper.

In the Gospel of Mark, Moses is on the mountain with Jesus, and so is Elijah.

These were two of the most pivotal characters in the Old Testament. In the tale of the transfiguration, Moses and Elijah are intended to represent the entirety of the law and the prophets of the Jewish faith. Moses and Elijah were pillars of Judaism. This is why the disciples asked if they should build shrines for Elijah and Moses too.

I think it is clear that the disciples still were clinging subconsciously to the traditions and teachings left by these two dead heroes.

However, Jesus often critiqued the laws and prophets in the Gospels. Jesus often accused Old Testament law and the teachings of the prophets of falling short in what God's children should aspire to become. We see this in Mark when Jesus says,

"You shall love the Lord your God with all your heart, and with all your soul, and with all your mind, and with all your strength.

> *The second is this: You shall love your neighbor as yourself. There is no other commandment greater than these."*

The text continues with a sentient cloud speaking to the disciples of Jesus by saying,

"This is my Son, listen to Him," and after this cloud instructed the disciples to honor the teachings of Jesus, they noticed that Moses and Elijah had vanished.

The sentient cloud in this story is incredibly similar in appearance to the transient fog representing YHWH (God) in the Old Testament that followed the nomadic Hebrews around and rested over the tabernacle that God instructed Moses to build when Moses was on Mount Sinai.

So the same mysterious cloud that represented God and followed Moses and the Jews while they wandered in the wilderness was now on the mountain before Jesus and the disciples.

What the story of the transfiguration of Jesus did was amazing.

The transfiguration was not written to dishonor the legacy of Moses and Elijah. It was a poetic way for the author of Mark to say that what Moses and Elijah did in the past was great for the faith, but what Jesus would do next would be even better. The author of Mark is conveying a belief that the movement of Jesus would be the next evolutionary step in humanity's eternal process of progress.

I am aware that I have been extremely hard on evangelicals this entire book, because the Christian faith has needed to make drastic changes for centuries. I do not regret any of my observations about fundamentalism in this document.

But that is not to say that everything in Christianity's past was horrible.

We have the capacity to celebrate positive moments in the timeline of Christian history, while also learning from our mistakes and encouraging the Church to take an evolutionary step forward that is long overdue.

What I adore about this passage in Mark is it gives a positive nod to founders of the faith while also acknowledging that, though Moses and Elijah were champions of progress, they were still far from perfect.

The great sage Capt. Malcolm Reynolds of the TV series *Firefly* said,

> *"Every person that has had a statue made of 'em was one kinda sumbitch or another."*

Do not read what I did not write. I think our integrity should be measured, and I believe our past matters. However, on the Church's path to progress perfection is the target we must aim for, knowing that we will miss it every time, but still we must try.

My desire for the Church is to admit that it is past time for us to strive to become better. The Church must endorse humanity's continued pursuit in the discovery of new scientific truths while helping society navigate our future with the ancient moral truths of love and justice. This is our calling, because God's story did not end with the Scriptures.

I think our gravest mistake in the history of Christianity was giving the Bible an ending. Humanity's understanding of the mechanics of the universe, and the shaping of morality here on Earth, is not a completed work. The Divine Mystery we call "God" still has revelations to be shared with all who are brave enough to seek new revelations for the Church.

On the mountain, in the valley, in the sky, in the ocean, in wild-life, in seasonal changes, in our depravity, and in our triumphs fingerprints of the Divine inspire, unfold, and explode within our experiences.

But religion, nationalism, xenophobia, racism, sexism, anti-Semitism, Islamophobia, transphobia, homophobia, capitalism, environmental destruction, and all other forms of intolerance are all remnants of a tarnished imperial faith that has crushed the Church's collective ambition for betterment.

I believe in spite of the enormous obstacles we face as a species, there is hope for humanity if we can resurrect the radical methods of a subversive Rabbi named Jesus.

The kingdom that Christ called "Heaven" has been before us and lies dormant within all neglected opportunities for virtuous action. An ethical world is and has always been possible. To see "Heaven" come to fruition requires only our collective willingness to bravely build a tomorrow that we believe can exist today.

So what can you do?

It is not up for me to answer that for you, but I can tell you that you won't find a brighter age in the methods of yesterday. The key to unlocking a utopian future cannot be found in a past that forged our semi-dystopian present. The answers to reshape our reality will only be revealed if we courageously ponder questions that have never been asked before.

Questioning is a byproduct of a faith that is actively searching for meaning and that is willing to take leaps to discover hidden secrets if necessary in order to blaze trails for a world that is lost.

Contrary to what chaplains of empire will tell you, being courageous enough to reexamine ancient knowledge, search for deeper meaning in the world around us, and ponder a just new age that benefits humanity equally is not weakness and it is certainly not heresy. This is the strongest system of faith that the world has ever seen. Those in seats of power know this. They tremble when revolutionaries dare to question why things are the way they are and why things have to be the way they have always been.

The two most dangerous words spoken to stagnant religious systems and imperious tyrants are:

"What if?"

Be brave enough to wield them, because there is no blueprint for innovation.

To quote Herman Melville in *Moby Dick:*

> *"It is not down on any map. True places never are."*

I truly believe that the most valuable currency we all possess is the treasure found within our own testimonies.

I began my faith journey and my career nourishing a bigoted, privileged, sexist, homophobic, hypocritical, and intolerant system of faith. This noxious religious institution creates followers that are simultaneously victims and victimizers in their communities. This travesty of spiritual death can no longer continue.

If the metaphorical message found in the resurrection of Jesus teaches us anything, it is that death, oppression, and destruction no longer belong, and they do not have the final word.

Transformation for the betterment of our world is not just possible. Manifesting it is a requirement for all who honor the legacy of Jesus.

If you no longer are sure of the relevance of Christendom, then I invite you to be reborn into a new reformation.

If you have been feeling that something is missing in your faith, then I invite you into a new existence that discards the influence of institutional tradition and religion.

If you sense that there is more to being a Christ follower than merely reciting a statement of faith concerning Christ's divinity, then I beckon you to be baptized into the nonviolent resistance that Jesus believed could bring Heaven to Earth.

Here.

Now.

Today.

Let us walk, hand in hand, in a mass exodus away from the clutches of evangelical manipulation that is masquerading itself as authentic Christianity. Help us reignite the radical renaissance of Jesus that Christendom intentionally abandoned centuries ago that the world desperately needs the Church to reclaim today.

I dare you. You won't regret it, and you'll never look back.

And now,

> *May the peace of the Radical Christ go with you,*
> *Wherever it may send you.*
> *May it guide you through the wilderness,*
> *protect you through the storm.*
> *May it bring you home rejoicing*
> *at the wonders that it has shown you.*
> *May it bring you home rejoicing*
> *once again into our doors.*

Grace and peace to you.

EPILOGUE

Years later, the church I came to plant in Santa Cruz has relaunched itself as Greater Purpose Community Church.

When we were dreaming about planting this new model we decided to ask ourselves,

"What pisses us off the most about Christianity?"

Out of that consistent meditation we fashioned a new type of community.

At Greater Purpose, our sermons incorporate conversation over adult beverages consumed in moderation. Parishioners can ask questions and make comments during the liturgy. Perhaps most importantly, we do not hold back in speaking up about the many injustices going on in American society that are being perpetuated by the Christian faith. As a community we are unashamed to demand better from both the Church and from our nation's leadership. We donate 50 percent of all tithes and offerings to local charities, we are open and affirming to LGBTQ people, we stand with Black Lives Matter, we stand for Native rights, we stand for feminism, we teach the importance of environmentalism and conservation, we teach spiritually minded folks not to be afraid of scientific discovery and to embrace evolution, and we also teach our congregation to live in harmony with differing faiths.

Recently we sold our church property to fund a new project. We are building a brewery that will donate up to 50 percent of all profits to local charities. After every purchase, customers will be able to select one of five local organizations to which they would like their funds to be allocated. They can choose between organizations like: Planned Parenthood, Save Our Shores, The Diversity Center, Homeless Garden Project, The NAACP, Native rights advocacy groups, recovery programs, and more.

All funds from this book will be allocated toward the start-up costs of our brewery venture. The story of how our brewery came to be will be the topic of my next book.

This community in Santa Cruz is a dream come true for me, but the exploration of new ways of "being church" cannot be isolated to a few congregations or followers of Christ in America.

Christianity's new reformation needs you.

Today.

So may you go forth and carve tomorrows chapter bravely. May you transform your community radically. May you shed the baggage of irrelevant tradition boldly. May you read the Scriptures in a way that promotes progress and that disables inequity. May you embrace the powerful initiatives of a subversive activist from Nazareth who stood against both temple and state, and may you be a living reminder to the Church of what it means to follow in the disruptive footsteps of a famous shit stirrer named Jesus.

P.S. Speaking of stirring shit up, with the exception of quotes and Bible verses, this entire book used gender neutral pronouns and as much inclusive language as possible.

Because when we are trying to reshape this world, our language matters.

Dammit!

FURTHER READING

If the thought, "Where the hell did Christopher come up with this shit?" entered your mind at any point in my book, then I invite you to check out these amazing literary works. I may not be totally on board with every theological position these authors have, but I have learned valuable information from each of these incredible works that inspired me at different points of my spiritual journey. More than a few of these books helped to shape the conclusions that I asserted in this book.

Jesus Interrupted and *The Triumph of Christianity* – Bart Ehrman

The Bible With Sources Revealed – Richard Elliot Friedman

What is The Bible, Jesus Wants to Save Christians, Sex God, What We Talk About When We Talk About God, Love Wins, and *Velvet Elvis* – Rob Bell

Jesus: A Revolutionary Biography – John Dominic Crossan

Blue Like Jazz, Searching for God Knows What, and *A Million Miles in a Thousand Years* – Donald Miller (These are great memoirs.)

Evolving in Monkey Town, A Year of Biblical Womanhood, and *Searching for Sunday* – Rachel Held Evans

The Myth of a Christian Nation, The Myth of a Christian Religion, and *God At War* – Gregory A. Boyd

Christianity After Religion and *A People's History of Christianity* – Diana Butler Bass

Insurrection – Peter Rollins

Pastrix, Accidental Saints, and *Shameless* – Nadia Bolz-Weber

We Make The Road by Walking it, A New Kind of Christian, A New Kind of Christianity, The Great Spiritual Migration, The Secret Message of Jesus, Naked Spirituality, and *Finding Faith: A Search for What Makes Sense* – Brian D. McLaren

Christ and the Caesars – Ethelbert Stauffer

Justification, Simply Christian, and *Surprised by Hope* – N. T. Wright

Excavating Jesus: Beneath the Stones, Behind the Texts – John Dominic Crossing and Jonathan L. Reed

Our Father Abraham – Marvin R. Wilson

The Ragamuffin Gospel – Brennan Manning

The Present Future, Missional Renaissance, and *Missional Communities* – Reggie McNeal

Jesus Against Christianity – Jack Nelson-Pallmeyer

The Liberation of Christmas – Richard A. Horsley

Follow me To Freedom, and *The Irresistible Revolution* – Shane Claiborne

SPECIAL THANKS

My Children: The three of you are the most precious gifts I have ever received. They say parenthood is akin to watching your heart leave your body and grow before your eyes. That doesn't come close to describing how much I adore you three. I will always cherish, support, and love each of you more than you can ever comprehend.

My Wife: I could not fulfill my calling without your patience and support. You are the most amazing person to enjoy life with. You are my soulmate. The eyes that I am most excited to see every morning are yours. You are my partner in crime for the rest of time. You are forever in my heart. "Always." (Yes that last part is a Harry Potter reference)

My Dogs: Albus and Ollivander (we really like Harry Potter), you bring me joy and entertainment. Thank you for keeping my feet warm while I typed this book at my desk. You are my fur babies and we are lucky to have rescued you both, because in a way you rescued us. If you two learn how to read one day, I hope you'll appreciate this shout out and the ridiculous cost of the grain-free organic dog food we spoil you with.

To the Mother of My Children: You and I may no longer be together, and I truly regret my former character flaws that contributed to that, but for what it is worth I truly appreciate all that you and your new partner do for our children. I am forever in your debt for that.

To My Grandfather: I miss you. Not a day goes by that I don't wish that I could see you. I still haven't measured up to the role model that you were for me, but your grand example of kindness will always be the standard I hold myself to. I love you and I'll always love you.

To Sean and Kristen: You are the family I chose. Without you I would have given up my ministry career long ago. I love you Sean, and your marriage to Kristen has always been a living example of my relationship goals. Never lose the love that makes others jealous of you both. Oh, and thank you for kicking me in the ass to start writing this book. There is a reason that you are both highlighted in it. Know that.

To Aundrea: I don't think anyone has ever had the privilege of understanding someone as clearly as you and I understand one another. I love our relationship. We are two personalities cut from the same cloth. I always have your back, no matter how rough and no matter the cost, because you have always had mine. Love ya amiga.

To Tripp: One of the memories I will take to my grave is the night we met. Talk about divine interference, am I right? We were destined to be close, my friend. I love and miss you every day. Now get your ass out to Cali, and give me a hug!

To Owen: I owe you my life. I try to live up to your moral fortitude on a consistent basis. Before I leave this world I wish to make an impact on one person that is as meaningful as what you did for me in my time of need. I miss you all the time. Especially our late night Bible conversations over a beer and a smoke.

To Jackson: I promise to never wait too long again. I should have joined the fray for racial equality sooner. Wherever you are in the next life my friend, save me a seat. We have lots to talk about when I get there. Rest in power.

To Jessica: There was a time when my world was falling apart and you were someone that held me together on more than one occasion. I can never thank you enough and could not love ya more. Bring bagels when ya visit.

To Tommy: To a great friend, a fun person to debate, a champion trivia partner, and the most tolerable Republican on the whole damn planet. I miss you, Bro Biden.

To Nico and Jess: To my friends that look exactly like the perfect couple in in newly purchased picture frames, I love you both to pieces. Save some pretty for the rest of us. Thank you for tolerating my obsession with your spouse Jess, but in truth I adore you both equally. (Don't tell Nico.)

To Mike: I count myself lucky to be working with you, and even more lucky to be your friend. Your beer-brewing skills kick serious ass and your ability to excel in most things blows my mind. We have only just begun, buddy! Buckle up, because your shenanigans are in my next book.

To Tina: Team awesome will ride again!

To GPCC: Who the hell would have thought we would be here? You are the example of what church should be and should have always been. I dreamt of y'all years before we started. Rarely do people get to live out their greatest ambitions. Never, ever, ever stop being the light that you all have become in Santa Cruz and to the world.

To Randall, Hannah, Christy, and Maria: So much of our story was made possible because of your sacrifice and willingness to innovate our new model. I will never forget you. Ever. Love y'all.

To Betty, Velma, Richard, and Pat: The sacrifices you all made to keep the Church alive for decades is worthy of eternal gratitude. Thank you for believing in me and for the bravery you had when we re-launched this church. You all cannot be commemorated enough.

To Richard: You are a rock star that has never gotten enough credit for the immeasurable value that you bring to the table. I love, appreciate, and respect you so much.

To Betty: You have given me more love and grace than I deserve. I adore you and Bob, and I am privileged to have y'all in the GPCC family.

To Gina: Thank you for teaching a better version of Christianity to our young ones than our generation received. You are a gift to the community.

To the Board, the Brewery Crew, The Band, and My Staff: Thanks for putting up with me and not having a mutiny … yet. You all are amazing.

To the Disciples of Christ: Thanks for showing me what home feels like. Here's to the best-kept secret in American Christianity. I have a feeling that the secret will get out soon.

To Rev. Dr. Bynum, Rev. Yolanda, and Rev Dan: If I become half the leaders y'all are, then I can die happy and I will leave a legacy of true leadership.

To Brian Mclaren: Thanks for pointing me in the right direction and taking the time to periodically speak words of encouragement to a young planter with lots of passion, crazy ideas, and zero credentials. Your work continues to give me life.

To Steve Knight: I don't tell you this often, but I look up to you more than any professional I know. I owe my career to your guidance. Keep fighting the good fight.

To my editors Barbara, Maria, and Roscher: Thank you for being awesome and for cleaning up my writing, CUZ I NO DO WORDS GOOD.

To Bernie and Veronica: Ali and I kinda want to be y'all when we grow up.

To Good Friends: Stacy, Raj, and Jenny, y'all will never leave my heart. I miss you all everyday. I love y'all.

To Santa Cruz: Let's hear it for the most beautifully weird place filled with the most wonderfully unique people in the world. Much love to the (831).

To Family: I know I am the "liberal nut job" of the bunch, but I am convinced that our family tree is a pecan tree because we're all a little nuts. I do love y'all dearly. Oh and #NotMyPresident.

To Those That Called Me Out: You are the real MVPs of this story. Keep melting hearts of stone. I owe you more than a few beers. Thank you so much.

To Evangelical Haters: Thank you for constantly reminding me that there is much more work to be done.

NOTES

CPSIA information can be obtained
at www.ICGtesting.com
Printed in the USA
FSHW011711040519
57853FS